It's Just A Matter of Time

Learning to Wait Patiently for God's Pre-ordained Plan To Materialize

*MS. Mary
Be Blessed*

By

Bishop Donald L. Smith

Bishop D. L. Sm

"It's Just a Matter of Time"

This book is dedicated to a true friend, encourager and
mentor, The Rev. Dr. Columbus Watson, Pastor of the
Beulah Baptist Church in Alexandria, Virginia.
He is a true mentor of preachers and a modern day
Barnabas (encourager) to all.
At a very trying and discouraging time in my ministry
when opportunities were few and far between he
provided me with opportunities, took time to teach me
one on one, and taught me many important principles
to the success in ministry. One of the most rewarding
principles he taught was *The 5 P's of Preaching* which
are: Privilege, Prayer, Preparation, Patience, and
Price. These principles if observed are sure tools for
sharpening the preacher's gift; for it is a man's gift that
will make room for him and bring him before great
men. Prov.18: 16.
"Young man" he said. "I see you one day in the future
teaching and training
Preachers."
Thank God for the prophets who speak destiny into
our lives. The prophecy has come to pass.
It Was Just A Matter Of Time!

Acknowledgments

A finished product is the sum total of toil, time, testing and tolerance of a number of dedicated people. I cannot begin to express my gratitude to those who God has set all around me in support of this tremendous project, my first book.

I'd like to first begin by thanking my Mother Louise D. Jones for raising me with a "can do" attitude. In the face of insurmountable odds she taught and modeled this attitude. *If you think you are, you are; if you think you can, you can.*

To my Pastor and Spiritual Father Dr. Frederick S. Jones of Star of Bethlehem Baptist Church, Triangle VA.

I am truly grateful for the opportunities you afforded me under your awesome leadership. The many lessons you taught all of your Sons of which I am proud to be "Number 47." You licensed me to preach the Glorious Gospel of Jesus Christ; It was you who ordained me into the pastorate. For these things I am truly grateful. Most of all, thanks for believing in me.

Secondly, my dear wife of 40 years, Meredith; you provide and maintain such a perfect home environment for one to write and think; yet while covering so many other task at the Church and school. Thanks for the extra encouraging push to finish. You truly are a Godsend! Much love.

To my Son and Elder Jerry Smith, administrative staff, and the intercessors at the Greater Mount Calvary Christian Church and The Whole Truth Ministries, Inc. Your support through this project has enabled me to keep my focus and not worry about the daytime operations or other ministry related task as things are done decently and in order with excellence and accuracy.

To my Daughter Unita, who chairs the Pastor and First Lady's Aide Ministry. One makes herself available to assist us in whatever task that is needful. You are a jewel and the best is yet to come for you.

Andrea, my Administrative Assistant. Your professional and expedient typing skills are just out of this world. Thanks for sacrificing and coming aboard our staff.

Last but not least, the "Faithful Few" of the Calvary leadership and family. Thanks! As God has enlarged my territory, and even through all of the challenges, you have been there for me exhibiting a ministering spirit and an attitude of encouragement and patience.

May God richly bless each of you is my prayer.

Contents

Introduction

How long wilt thou forget me, O lord? Forever?
How long wilt thy hide thy face from me?
How long shall I take counsel in my soul, having
sorrow in my heart daily? How long shall mine
enemy be exalted over me?

Psalm 13:1-2

"How long"? This question is repeated no less than four times in the text. It embodies the very intense desire for immediate attention or deliverance with great anguish of heart. I might add that there is a bit of impatience and frustration detected in these interrogatives. But is this not the true portrait of our very own experiences?

It's not always easy to prevent desire from degenerating to impatience; impatience to frustration and frustration to anguish. Pray God that while we're waiting on deliverance we be kept from indulging in a murmuring and complaining spirit which God himself despises.

My dear reader, have you ever been waiting on God for an answer to a prayer; deliverance from a terrible situation, direction for your travel, a solution to a problem, a resolution to a dilemma?

Often times we feel like the Psalmist in this "how long song". To encourage us, others constantly remind us of another encouraging word from the same Psalmist in Psalm 30:5. We all have heard it at one time or another.

"Weeping may endure for a night but joy comes in the morning." But our response is "Oh Lord. I know that your word is true and I do believe that joy comes in the morning; but Lord could you just answer one question for me; how long is the night?

Does your conversation with God sound like the following one?

"Lord you gave me a vision of my breakthrough and promised it would surely come to pass and not lie and I should just wait for it. But it seems that I'm still stuck in this perpetual holding pattern. As I circumference this same mountain over and over again with deliverance nowhere in sight; O Lord, How much longer? Have you forgotten me? How long will you hide your face from me?

Lord I don't mean to be disrespectful and I'm certainly not questioning your authority; but if you would just give me a sign, or just reveal to me the method of this madness; your master plan, your divine strategy.

O Lord, all I'm asking is for a divine impartation or a revelation from you. As a dear pants for water, my soul thirsts for you. I need to draw from your vast reservoir of knowledge, wisdom and intellectual resources. I'm in need of a supernatural exchange.

I've come to the end of my rope, the extent of my patience, and the depth of my understanding. Lord how long? How much longer must I suffer, must I cry myself to sleep at night, must I be lonely. How long must I continue to tolerate people hurting me? How long must I be misunderstood, unappreciated and go through these elongated periods of confusion?

It seems like even my wicked neighbors prosper and the hypocrites seem to get all the blessings, but the true saints go without. Lord how long?

My Bishop keeps telling me it's going to be alright after while, just keep hanging in there for this too will come to pass. Lord. I'm tired of hearing that! Please tell me why is my blessing being delayed?

He also tells us to do a self-critique and I have; Well, I'm faithful in church attendance, Bible study, prayer and praise service. Not only do I tithe but I also give offerings, first fruit, sew seed and serve on two ministries. I treat my neighbor right but forgive those who trespass against me. I'm not perfect Lord you know that, but I also ask forgiveness for my shortcomings. But the truth is I'm discouraged and frustrated with the pace of things in my life. No, I'm not about to quit, give up or backslide, get high or surrender to temptation or the lusts of this world, but God I'm on my knees and I just want a preview...how much longer?

How much longer do I wait for my vision to manifest? Lord I'm sending up a SOS. This is a 911 call. I desperately need a breakthrough!

Not another second, not another minute, not another hour of another day. Lord I need you now, right away!"

My friend, maybe your heart speaks the very sentiments of all the words of the scenario above. Perhaps you've been bewildered, confused or discouraged while waiting on God. You're wondering why your vision tarries, your breakthrough is on hold and your efforts seem fruitless. Why is it taking so long for the dawn of your morning to arrive or your change to spring forth?

Well, I don't have all the answers; but I can tell you that I've been there, and done that! God spoke to me some time ago when I presented this same case before his majesties' royal court. In a still small voice, He said. *"Be patient... it's just a matter of time."*

It's Just a Matter of Time
1. And all the congregation lifted up their voice and cried; and the people wept all that night.

2. And all the children of Israel murmured against Moses and against Aaron: and the whole congregation said unto them, would God that we had died in the land of Egypt! Or would God that we died in the wilderness!

3. And wherefore hath the Lord brought us into this land, to fall by the sword, that our wives and our children should be a prey? Was it not better for us to return into Egypt?

4. And they said one to another, let us make a captain, and let us return into Egypt.

5. Then Moses and Aaron fell on their faces before all the assembly of the congregation of the children of Israel.

6. And Joshua the son of Nun, and Caleb the son of Jephunneh, which were of them that searched the land, rent their clothes:

Numbers 14: 1-6

God's Eternal Existence

Psalm 90:2
*Before the mountains were brought forth, or even
thou hadst formed the earth and the world, even from
everlasting to everlasting, thou art God.*

One of the things that I've become acutely aware of in this
stage of my ministry is how essential it is that we teach and
minister in the body of Christ the whole truth; especially as it
relates to the timing of the Lord.

The promises of God are certain so we spend a lot of time
teaching on the promises so that the people become excited about
what is their spiritual and physical heritage in the kingdom and
the after life. (Heaven)

The problem that causes us to digress from complete success
in that arena is that we fail to equip the body in regard to proper
theology as it relates to God's timing.

God is a God of order and sequence. He's a God of methods.
He does not move haphazardly or chaotically even though He
moves in the midst of chaotic situations.

We must understand the methodology of the Holy Spirit;
learn to wait and move only when He grants us the grace to do
so.

So in order to bring about a greater understanding of God's
moving among His people I want to offer you some biblical
principles.

We must understand that God exist in eternity. There are no birthdays for God. He doesn't get old, tired, or weary because He exists in eternity. God is a spirit and must be worshiped in spirit and truth. Eternity is older than time. "From everlasting to everlasting thou art God." He lives in eternity.

Now He created time as a module for man to dwell in. Genesis tells us that the evening and the morning was the first day. So He's the author of the first day, the first second, the first minute, the first hour and called it time; but He created time for man. So man lives in time and God dwells in eternity.

All the decrees and mandates of God are decreed and mandated in eternity. It's called pre-destination. The destiny of everything and person is pre-determined before it's existence and eventually by God's grace and our submission to His plan they manifest in time.

It's only a matter of time before that which God has pre-determined will be revealed in time.

The Bible tells us in Revelation 13: 8 that the Lamb was slain before the foundation of the world. He was slain in eternity before time. I'm glad to know today that in eternity the sin issue was settled before it was even started. God settled it in eternity and manifested it in time. He revealed a lamb in time and called it Jesus, who was already slain from the foundations of the world.

So because God exists in eternity and you're praying in time, often times you're praying, toiling, worrying in time about things that God has already settled in eternity. And He knows that it's only a matter of time before He reveals what He's already decreed in eternity.

Now eternity transcends time, it supercedes time and exists apart and outside of time; so God can make statements like He is the same yesterday, today, and forevermore.

Now this doesn't only mean that He never changes. It's much deeper than that. It also means He stands outside of time and looks at time from an eternal position. He can be the same yesterday, today and forevermore.

This also means He can see where I am, where I was, and where I will be in one glance. My past, my present and my future are all locked into his peripheral vision.

I can pray about something now that hurt me then but He can take a word that He gives me now and reach back into my then and heal my yesterday, so I can be free today and loose for my tomorrow.

Jesus Christ. He's the great I AM. I AM He which is, which was, and is to come. I AM—I am then, now and forevermore—I AM God and beside there is no other.

In the 90th Psalm Moses from a poetic perspective writes and attempts to define His existence; but he came to the resolve and said from everlasting to everlasting thou art God; sovereign, absolute and completely in control.

In Psalm 31:15 from a revelation of God's sovereignty David makes the supporting proclamation when he stated "my times are in His hands."

The Significance of Time

Psalm 90:12
So teach us to number our days, that we may apply our hearts to unto wisdom.

Time was created for man as an agent for purpose. Ecclesiastes 3:1 says for everything there is a time and season for every purpose under Heaven.

So time is given to me so that I can appreciate how far I am in regard to my purpose. In other words the amount of days I've been here. Have I used these days to fulfill my purpose?

Then time becomes an instrument for me to monitor my success; for me to be able to determine for all of my days, have I done what he's called me to do? And if I have done what he's called me to do—then I am successful. Whether I live up to anyone else's standards or expectations becomes immaterial. As long as I have done what God has predestined for me to do. That's why I can never be fulfilled until I get in touch with the creator and ask him for what purpose was I created? And when I understand my purpose and walk in it. It's only then can I determine if I've been successful or not.

One can have access to a lot people, possessions, fame, and finance and still not be successful. If I fail to do what He's divinely created me to do and to accomplish, then I then become a failure as it pertains to my earthly mission and assignment.

So that's why God continues to gives us time and chance, after chance, after chance. That we might know Him and respond to His call of sanctification on our lives; then know our purpose and become successful as we walk in it.

Hebrews 11: 3

Through faith we understand that the worlds were framed
by the word of God, so that things which are seen were
not made of things which do appear.

The mystery of this text lies in the word "worlds"...the word worlds in the Greek is not *cosmos* which means planet, but it is *ions* which means ages.

Through faith we understand that the ages were framed by the word of God. The times, ages, ions, even dispensations were all framed by the word of God. That means God spoke a word that progressively went forth out of his mouth. The Holy Scripture refers to it as *the proceeding word. The* proceeding word of God is an ongoing, eternal, and everlasting word. And as it went out it framed in or scheduled my times, my future, and my destiny. When God speaks, His word will not just stop but it continues and will not return void. Isaiah 55:11

So when the Elohim said let there be light on one day it didn't stop on that day. It was a perpetual-continuing-ongoing-infusion of light into the darkness that framed light down through the ions of time, therefore light has never needed to be re-created.

And the word said as long as it takes I'll keep on going until I've accomplished what God has pre-destined. For He has commanded it and He is God!!!

Bound by Time:

God began the measurement of time on the 4th creative day when He made the sun & moon (Gen.1:14). Not only are we affected daily by the appearance & disappearance of the sun, the changes of the moon affecting tides - always on a repeating, regular basis, but also within our own body there are many timed events (regular heart rate & breathing, need for food & elimination, & sleep just to name a few). We are on a schedule of time. God is so busy & active, time is perceived much differently than us.

For a thousand years in thy sight are but as yesterday when it is past, and as a watch in the night. Psa.90:4;

But, beloved, be not ignorant of this one thing, that one day is with the Lord as a thousand years, and a thousand years as one day. 2 Peter 3:8

1000 years as a day. Or

24 hrs. = 1000 yrs.
12 hrs. = 500 yrs.
1 hr. = 41.67 yrs.
1 min. = .694 of a yr. (253.3 days)
1 sec. = 4.22 days

Our Time is Important to God:

Rom 13:11-13 *And that, knowing the time, that now it is high time to awake out of sleep: for now is our salvation nearer than when we believed. The night is far spent, the day is at hand: let us therefore cast off the works of darkness, and let us put on the armour of light.*

Knowledge of our time, being aware of ourselves in 'God's plan', provides for an armour of light meaning 'we can see!' (1Jn.1:5 God is Light - Gen.1:3 Let there be God!). Let's look at each 'time' reference in Rom.13:11-13:

Knowing the time: Don't keep avoiding God, avoiding truth, by blaming others & making excuses. Know your time, right now - salvation or damnation are very near; - face it & don't run;

Jn 5:39-40 *Search the scriptures; for in them ye think ye have eternal life: and they are they which testify of me. And ye will not come to me, that ye might have life.*

Some 'think' they are saved when they are not, & they continually avoid the truth.

Heb.11:1 we are taught to have 'now faith', 'current' faith, updated, in tune with the times, present (not past), now faith.

It is high time: or it has come to the ultimate peak of timing to wake up & get right with God. This 'sleep' is not a relaxing unconscious state - it is a spiritual blindness, spiritually unconscious state (Eph.4:18).

Now: Pay attention to right now! Stop bringing up the past (using it for excuses) & worrying about the future. Matt.6:33-34.

Salvation is nearer than you think: we have thoughts about many things that are opposite to God. Isa.55:8-9 Be aware of the mess we made with wrong thinking before God led us to truth. Salvation is nearer because you don't know how God is taking you: death or rapture.

3 types of "time" to consider;

1) Jesus is coming soon & those unprepared will be left behind. (Luke 21:28)
2) Some may face death very soon - again, the unprepared will be left behind; (Luke 12:20)
3) Then there are the scariest people - those whose sin & decisions make it possible God may cut them off real soon, except they repent. (Rom.1:28)

Night is far spent: So many have wasted so much time, fooling around chasing carnal goals. The night time of sin is ending soon & many people see & feel it while many are asleep. No-one can stop or delay it - the night of sin is almost over & great tribulation is on the doorstep. Do you know the times? Your time is almost up!

God Is the Steward of His Word

Jeremiah 1:12
Then said the Lord unto me, Thou hast well seen:
for I will hasten my word to perform it.

God watches over His word (being alert and active)to perform it…to uphold it—sustain it— by the word of His power.

Now I understand why I'm still here. I've been begotten by the word of God. The same word that spoke me into existence is holding me up. Heb. 1:3. That's why when I'm operating in God's will; no weapon formed against me, shall able to prosper.

Even when I wanted to come down the power of His word upheld me. Even when I feel like quitting I can't. There's something that keeps me in the race. Often tired but I'm still going. Broke- busted—often disgusted—but still going.

I've been through a whole lot of things that should have taken me out but I'm still going. My critics said I wouldn't last two years; but 26 years have passed since that fatal prophecy was given and I'm still going. Many prophesied I'd have a heart attack, but I'm still going. The enemy even tried to food poison me. But I'm still going.

They called in their witches and warlocks but I'm still going. Cast their spells, spoke their incantations but I'm still going… threaten to put me out but I'm still going— death threats – and heart breaking desertion… but I'm still standing.

That's my miracle. I'm still going! A whole lot of folk would have folded; but I know the Lord is with me for my enemies have not destroyed me. I'm still living, surviving, maintaining, progressing, praising, preaching and prophesying.

I'm holding on to my faith in God in spite of the tremendous suffering. I still believe Him.

There are nights I've cried after giving the best of my love, care and counsel to end up being deserted, misused, and abused by the very one's I hoped to help. Yes I've been through the fire and the flood but it's now after all of that I can truly say "I know He framed in my future." It's only now that I truly understand what it means to be Predestined. A chosen one; and when you're chosen you're not perfect in your walk, neither or exempt from troubles, but chosen. When God has found favor in you, He underwrites your mission and guarantees your success.

God's favor and His enabling grace is upon you. Thank God He favored me!

It's amazing, even when we get out of line, wanting to do our own thing, leaning to our own understanding He pulls us back in line. Often times we fall down but He picks us back up and holds us together.

I'm sure many of you reading this can relate. When you think you're having a nervous breakdown or about to lose your mind and if one more thing happened you really would have flipped out; But God was in the midst holding you together.

Really on the edge sometimes, but I discovered so was He; right there to uphold me! So my times are absolutely, positively in His hands. It truly makes a difference whose hands you're in. I encourage you to cast your cares upon Him and put it all in His hands.

So it's only a matter of time until that which God has predestined and predetermined happens in my life.

That's why I can wait on the Lord and be of good courage. (Psalm 27:14)

I've learned to sit like Forrest Gump at the bus stop and patiently tell my story. I know the bus is coming. I don't always see it, or hear it, but I must wait with expectation and know it's just a matter of time before it arrives.

So when you operate by this principle, it impacts and transforms your thinking.

Now you come to church for different reasons than those who don't realize this truth. You no longer come for sociological entanglements. You don't necessarily come looking for friendship because your perspective is different.

That's one reason you should never leave a good church for the (bad) people who are in it. They shouldn't bother you because you didn't come to see them anyway.

When you discover that church folk, just like you aren't perfect, just forgiven; and many are yet searching for their place in God and His Kingdom. Then your entire perspective changes; It's then that our request is like that of the Grecian worshippers in John 12: 20. "Sirs, we would see Jesus."

You come to hear from Him and to get your soul fed!

You're hungry for something to make you hold on until what he's framed up—predestined for you begins to manifest and come to pass.

I come to feed my faith so I can see into my future.

I pay my tithes so a window in heaven opens and I can see my future, my destiny—my stuff. Just as the Hebrew writer says, "Jesus endured the cross for the joy that was on other side." We too must endure our temptations and trials in order to arrive at the other side of through.

Therefore, to get through my experience I must do what it takes for me to endure. I shout, cry, get happy, suffer, sacrifice and endure for it's all about what He's framed up and kept in storage for me. The sufferings of this present time are not worthy to be compared with the glory which shall be revealed in us. Romans 8:18

Personal Commitment

Philippians 4:13
I can do all things through Christ which strengthens me.

Whatever I was created to do, whatever my destiny may be or my future holds, if I expect to realize it, I and I alone must make a decision to be committed to reaching my goals and doing daily what it takes to get me through one day at a time.

John C. Maxwell in his book *Today Matters* writes "in order to become the person you have the potential to be, you will need great tenacity. That quality comes from commitment."

He further quotes Frederick F. Flash in *Choices* "Most people can look back over the years and identify a time and place at which their lives changed significantly. Whether by accident or design, these are the moments when, because of readiness within us a collaboration with events occurring around us, we are forced to seriously reappraise ourselves and the conditions under which we live and to make certain choices that will affect the rest of our lives".

Look back over the events of your life and recall when you made a heartfelt commitment to do something differently; your life changed as a result of that decision. It may have not turned out exactly as you wanted or expected but it definitely set your life on a new course. If we want to experience change, commitment must be at the heart of each decision we make.

Commitment is the one tool that helps us to overcome many of life's obstacles. We all have problems. The question is, how are you going to deal with them?

One of the most common mistakes and one of the costliest is thinking that success is due to some genius, some magic formula or power that we do not posses.

As we observe the successful people before our time or even our contemporaries, we must not begin to think that their fire is hotter and their ice is colder but realize that success is generally due to holding on to a vision and refusing to let go until you see the manifestation of it.

Statistics show that the majority of people who fail don't fail because of the lack of vision, resources or support...they fail because of a loss of focus and a lack of commitment.

Whatever task you decide to undertake be it to learn a new language, study music, take a course in reading, writing a book or training yourself physically. The factor which will determine if it will be a success or failure is the level of commitment that you possess to see your project come to fruition. That level that projects the attitude of a winner which says "nothing will overrule my decision, and nothing will detach my grip, I will hold on until I reach my goal." This will bring success.

You must understand on your road to success you will encounter many fatal attractions that will have the propensity to become distractions and without a high level of commitment and focus these distractions will become infractions to separate you from the heart of your vision and the fatal end is a loss of focus and another unfinished project.

It is these two all important ingredients; focus and commitment that actually fuels your vision. I am reminded of Jesus (John 4:4) while on a mission to Samaria... The writer states his vision and the importance of it when he says *he must needs to go through Samaria*".

After meeting the Samaritan woman at the well, and a lengthy conversation... Jesus took his time to effectively minister to her for He transformed her thinking and sent her on a mission. The end results were the whole city came to see Him.

Meanwhile the disciples urged Him to eat something, but He assured them "I have food- nourishment-fuel to eat that you know not of"...then He explained. "My food/nourishment is to do the will of He who sent me and to finish/accomplish His work."

Your Commitment Will Be Tested and Tried by Fire

I Peter 4:12
Beloved, think it not strange concerning the fiery trial which is to try you, as though some strange thing happened unto you:

Many people today are confused for they have been deceived to think that commitment is an event, something that is done in a moment. You witness them saying "I do" in a wedding ceremony, they shake hands to close a business deal. They even buy a membership to their local gym or buy a treadmill to exercise, but they fail to recognize the fact that commitment doesn't end with that decision; it's just getting started. And you best believe that any time you make a commitment to something, it will be tested and tried. This happens in various ways:

*Fear of Failure: One of the greatest challenges to commitment is the fear of failure. All of us want to be successful...we have big dreams. We all try to achieve them; but on our way to achieving those dreams, if we face failure, we just totally break down. Often after we experience failure we lose the courage to pursue our goal because of the failure we faced in the previous attempt.

Consciously or unconsciously, the fear of failure affects our performance.

As we observe the disciple Peter in Matthew 14: 28 requesting to walk on water to Jesus, he was granted the permission by Jesus himself to "Come". Peter begin to walk on the water but when he saw the boisterous wind and waves he became afraid and begin to sink; But he didn't give up but requested help from the one who gave him permission to walk on the water. He tried again after receiving a second affirmation for divine assistance and he walked back to the ship.

In his book *Failing Forward* John Maxwell says "All achievers have in common the ability to bounce back after an error, mistake or a failure." He quotes Psychologist Simone Caruthers- "Life is a series of outcomes. Sometimes the outcome is what you want. Great. Figure out what you did right. Sometimes the outcome is what you don't want. Great. Figure out what you did wrong so you don't do it again." That's the key to bouncing back.

Achievers are able to keep moving forward no matter what happens. And that's made possible because they remember that failure does not make them *failures*. No one should take mistakes personally. That's the way to take yourself out of a failure.

*Multiple Distractions: As aforementioned in the previous chapter men don't fail because of lack of vision or provision but the loss of focus. Whenever you are in serious pursuit of a goal you must be prepared to deal with distractions. They will come in the form of:

People
Places
Possessions
Positions

These things will challenge you. Yes, they will even tempt you to compromise your values and prostitute your righteous principles.

In these trying times you must ask yourself the question "who am I trying to please?" If the resolve is to first please God and then yourself by following through on your commitments you must then be prepared to stand alone.

When Satan wants to distract you he will inject one of the above tools into your life to break your focus or hinder you from the call and assignment God has ordained for your life. So Jesus, the *Author and Finisher of our Faith*, even our destiny; in His incredible wisdom knows how to remove those distractions and cause us to behold Him again. Keep your focus …Look unto Him.

*Facing Disappointment: We must be honest. As we are in righteous pursuit of our vision and goals the scripture lets us know in Psalm 34:19 –*Many are the afflictions of the righteous; but the Lord delivers us from them all.*

Secondly, we must also consider what we know as Murphy's law: "whatever can go wrong, will go wrong".

How will you respond or react in the face of disappointments. Things go wrong, life gets tough, pain is a reality, sickness is inevitable, and death is unavoidable but how do you keep going in the face of it all? If you determine to make and keep proper commitments daily, you greatly improve your chances of being able to carry on, move forward and complete your assignment.

The Necessity of Church

Hebrews 10:24-25
And let us consider one another to provoke
unto love and to good works:
Not forsaking the assembling of ourselves together, as the manner
of some is; but exhorting one another: and so much more, as ye
see the day approaching.

When one truly has a sense of the calling on his or her life they cannot afford to be deceived like so many others in this season thinking that they don't need church. I would like to take this opportunity to inform those who are of this dangerous ilk. Jesus calls us into separation but not isolation. You need a spiritual covering and connection.

Church is the place I belong and I must realize if I'm not connected and in faithful attendance in a local church as I'm able (the body of Christ) I am out of fellowship. Therefore my access to the power and anointing of God is limited.

The scripture emphatically admonishes us in Heb. 10:24-25... not to forsake the assembling of ourselves together as believers as is the habit of some people. But admonishing and encouraging one another all the more as we see the day approaching... that we may give attentive, continuous care to one another; studying how we might stir up love, and provoke one another to helpful deeds and noble activates. That's the benefit of fellowship.

12 Reasons Why Church Membership Matters

Jonathan Leeman in "The Leadership Journal" gives us some awesome insight as to why church membership matters.

He states that *"Membership is the church's affirmation that you are a citizen of Christ's kingdom and therefore a card-carrying Jesus Representative before the nations."*

(The following is excerpted from Jonathan Leeman's forthcoming book Why Church Membership? *from Crossway, 2012.)*

1) *It's biblical.* Jesus established the local church and all the apostles did their ministry through it. The Christian life in the New Testament is church life. Christians today should expect and desire the same.

2) *The church is its members.* To be "a church" in the New Testament is to be one of its members (read through Acts). And you want to be part of the church because that's who Jesus came to rescue and reconcile to himself.

3) *It's a pre-requisite for the Lord's Supper.* The Lord's Supper is a meal for the gathered church, that is, for members (see 1 Cor. 11:20, 33). And you want to take the Lord's Supper. It's the team "jersey" which makes the church team visible to the nations.

4) *It's how to officially represent Jesus.* Membership is the church's affirmation that you are a citizen of Christ's kingdom and therefore a card-carrying Jesus Representative before the nations. And you want to be an official Jesus Representative. Closely related to this...

5) *It's how to declare one's highest allegiance.* Your membership on the team, which becomes visible when you wear the "jersey," is a public testimony that your highest allegiance belongs to Jesus. Trials and persecution may come, but your only words are, "I am with Jesus."

6) *It's how to embody and experience biblical images.* It's within the accountability structures of the local church that Christians live out or embody what it means to be the "body of Christ," the "temple of the Spirit," the "family of God," and so on for all the biblical metaphors

(see 1 Cor. 12). And you want to experience the interconnectivity of his body, the spiritual fullness of his temple, and the safety and intimacy and shared identity of his family.

7) *It's how to serve other Christians.* Membership helps you to know which Christians on Planet Earth you are specifically responsible to love, serve, warn, and encourage. It enables you to fulfill your biblical responsibilities to Christ's body (for example, see Eph. 4:11-16; 25-32).

8) *It's how to follow Christian leaders.* Membership helps you to know which Christian leaders on Planet Earth you are called to obey and follow. Again, it allows you to fulfill your biblical responsibility to them (see Heb. 13:7; 17).

9) It *helps Christian leaders lead.* Membership lets Christian leaders know which Christians on Planet Earth they will "give an account" for (Acts 20:28; 1 Peter 5:2).

10) *It enables church discipline.* It gives you the biblically prescribed place to participate in the work of church discipline responsibly, wisely, and lovingly (1 Cor. 5).

11) *It gives structure to the Christian life.* It places an individual Christian's claim to "obey" and "follow" Jesus into a real-life setting where authority is actually exercised over us (see John 14:15; 1 John 2:19; 4:20-21).

12) *It builds a witness and invites the nations.* Membership puts the alternative rule of Christ on display for the watching universe (see Matt. 5:13; John 13:34-35; Eph. 3:10; 1 Peter 2:9-12). The very boundaries which are drawn around the membership of a church yield a society of people which invites the nations to something better.

So faithful church attendance, participation and partnership (fellowship) is a priority. But it also matters where you go to church.

Places matter to God. You see the Creator made specific places before He even made people.

The first known assignment of the Holy Spirit in creation was to a specific place...the face of the waters (Gen. 1:2)

On the day of Pentecost the Holy Spirit was scheduled to appear and reveal Himself in a specific place... An upper room(Acts 1: 2-4)

Jesus scheduled miracles to occur in specific places ...in Samaria-(John 4:4)

The instruction of Jesus to a blind man to receive his sight was to a specific place...the pool of Siloam (John 9:7)

Namaman, the leper, was instructed by the prophet to dip seven times in a specific place...the Jordan River (11 Kings 5:10)

Elijah was instructed to go to a specific place for supernatural provision. Zarephath (1 Kings 17 4; 9)

Brethren please be careful and prayerful. For rebellion to enter a place of obedience always produces tragic results...(ie... Jonah)

As it relates to your financial breakthrough, spiritual enrichment and elevation, nothing is more important than the place where you have been assigned. It's there God has scheduled you enter into tutelage, discipleship, partnership and the fellowship of others to mature and position you to receive the fullness of His blessings.

Some places may seem uncomfortable for they challenge and cause you to leave your comfort zone. That's where you want to be! Yes, you want to go where the preacher /prophet speaks to your issues like He's in your business.

You wonder who's called him and told him what's going on in your life?

To be honest you know the preacher doesn't know anything about you or your situation but you must receive it; not as a coincidence, but God ordering your footsteps that you might receive answers to your questions, solutions to your problems and direction for your journey.

Flourishing In Your Set Place

1 Corinthians 12:18
But now hath God set the members every one of them
in the body, as it hath pleased Him.

We must be careful to note that the scripture says "everyone". Not every other or some; but *everyone* has been set in the body as it pleases Him. This let's us know that we are significant in the plan of God. He has meticulously set every member in the body.

Not only the local church but also in the life of your pastor for the purpose of maturing, mentoring, and being fed with all wisdom and knowledge so that you can become an intricate part of the vision of the house; especially after you're promoted to leadership positions. You then become a key factor in what God wants to do in the local body of your assignment. Jeremiah 3:15

Understanding that you are a key factor in what God is going to do and you must take the awesome responsibility of submitting and grounding yourself. Remember. You can't quit because of what is happening to you or around you when things are not pleasing to you! That my friend is a demonic decoy. The scripture teaches you were set in the body as it pleases God; not yourself or any other friend or family member.

If you become deceived and abort your mission or abandon your assignment not only do you, delay your destiny. But there is also a danger of aborting your inheritance.

Some might say "but Bishop you don't know what's happening!" To be frank, I don't need to know. There is one thing I do know and that is that the anointing of God will keep you in any and all adverse circumstances.

Case and point: David and King Saul — —Saul disliked David after he became popular with the people. He despised him and even threatened his life by throwing javelins at him. But David slipped from his presence twice and continued in service without one desire for revenge. The Bible says David conducted himself wisely in all of his ways and continued to serve his King. The Lord was with him and Saul became afraid of David and promoted him to captain over thousands of soldiers. David refused to be driven from his set place of duty even though life-threatening adversity surrounded him.

Often time on your journey to destiny you will experience distasteful moments; but if you magnify them you will play right into the enemies' hands and he will apply pressure in order to push, pull, or lure you out of your set place of blessing.

In my assignment as pastor and overseer I observe many things that are displeasing to me. Why? Because I know that they are displeasing to God. Especially when the members of a body take communion and covenant with God and each other to support the local body physically, financially, and spiritually but it does not always happen. Covenants are broken and yes it's frustrating; but it no wise releases me from my God given assignment.

It's only when I remain faithful and focused that I am exposed to a strength and a level of God's grace I would have never experienced if I had quit and thrown in the towel. His grace is sufficient!

Many may ask the question what is a set place. Is it literal, physical and is it scriptural? The answer is yes to each of these questions.

I do pray the characteristics and descriptions listed below will be helpful to you in defining a set place.

1. A set place is a spiritual place; a place where God has ordained that I dwell for the purposes of maturity.

A place of total submission to His order; for when my ways pleases the Lord He will make my enemies at peace with me.   Proverbs 16: 7

So my set place is a place ordained by God. It's spiritual, mental, physical, and relational; whereby a person of destiny lives out the purposes and plans of God and finds ultimate fulfillment in life.

Therefore we've been created by God and ordained to do a specific work (Eph. 2:10) and one must understand that he is not going to be fulfilled until he is doing what God has set him in the earth to do.

God hides our fulfillment in His plan and we only experience it when we begin to do what He has created and ordained us to do in this earth realm.

2. A place of connection through God sent righteous relationships that God has for me.

3. An attitude that God has designed for me (Philp. 2:5-8)

4. A certain geographical location God has assigned to me; a city, area, Church, or ministry within a church.

5. A mindset; a mental state of abundance and not lack; place of submission.

So we begin to submit ourselves to His plan and follow Him obediently step-by-step, moment-by-moment. It is then that we discover the fulfillment that He has for us.

The Power of Agreement

Numbers 14:5-6
Then Moses and Aaron fell on their faces before all the
assembly of the congregation of the children of Israel.
And Joshua the son of Nun, and Caleb the son of
Jephunneh, which were of them that searched
the land, rent their clothes.

Here we see Moses and Aaron falling on their faces while Joshua and Caleb are tearing their garments. Why?

While on the path to your promise land and you discover that you're associated with people that you are not connected to. This situation will make you rent your garments. The act of renting garments is a sign of shame and awesome frustration.

When you continue to walk with people and see the same things but they see it differently and speak negative comments. It will make you rent your garments.

I prefer to keep my distance from pessimistic folk —telling me what I can't accomplish or what I can't possess.

I don't even want to come to church to get discouraged—I was discouraged before I arrived at church.

I do desire that people with faith- vision- and hope, circumference me. This kind of company is most encouraging and a divine source of empowerment.

Jesus teaches us in Matt. 18: 19- 20"...*that if any two persons shall agree on earth as touching, anything that they ask shall be done for them of the heavenly Father which is in heaven.*

For where two are three are gathered together in my name, there am I in the midst of them."

I truly believe the progress of many believers today is gridlocked and they are experiencing high levels of frustration, exhaustion and spiritual burnout because of this very important factor.

They're touching (associated) with folk who are not in agreement with them.

If so, this type of relationship is unhealthy for it's nature is to pull you down, by tearing at the very fiber of your faith. You'll soon become exhausted and cast down because of so much frustration. You begin to wonder if it's worth it. Please accept this bit of counsel. No! It is not worth it.

It's a negative draw upon your spirit to have people with you and not be of the same mind. It's difficult to have any true fellowship with them because they're disconnected from the vision that you have in your spirit.

It is imperative to befriend those that you can touch and agree with.

It's a terrible thing to be fixed in a frustrating and pessimistic environment. That's bad ministry. It's truly a struggle to survive let alone thrive and be productive.

In chapter two of his book "Maximize The Moment" Bishop T.D. Jakes speaks of Predators and Partners. He says (quote) "We are not solitary creatures. Every day we interact with countless numbers of people...God does not means for us to be alone. We are meant to live and work together and obviously we are stronger in numbers. Joint efforts usually yield better results.

To be most effective, we should come together, share our talents, motivate each other, and profit from the joyous unity of like-minded individuals who share their skills, hearts, and lives.

However, not all relationships serve to benefit us. There are some relationships that should be avoided; they sap your life away and weaken your focus. If you are going to maximize your life, you need to recognize these toxic relationship and know when to walk away from them. We must be vigilant about the company we keep and learn to sever those ties that strangle us, associations that are filled with turmoil, affiliations that need continuous maintenance, and alliances

that undermine.

A toxic relationship can be like a bad leg that is gangrenous. If you don't amputate it, the infection will spread throughout your entire body.

The bitter bile of one bad relationship can seep into every other aspect of your life. It can destroy your family, bankrupt your business, and blacken your heart. People who do not have the courage to cut off what will not heal will eventually end up losing so much more."

Accepting the challenge

1 Samuel 17: 28
And Eliab his eldest brother heard when he spake unto the men; and Eliab's anger was kindled against David, and he said, Why camest thou down hither? and with whom hast thou left those few sheep in the wilderness? I know thy pride, and the naughtiness of thine heart; for thou art come down that thou mightest see the battle.

Are you up for the challenge? The greatest challenge is to have the anointing to be King and go back out there to the shepherd's field. To go back down to the base things and take that strong anointing and still tend sheep and not allow what God has given you by post-date to depress you where you are right now. Beloved don't become frustrated. God has given you a preview of coming attractions.

Don't let the vision frustrate you, because you can't do in your flesh what is going to take time for God to develop and process the spiritual maturity in your life.

He didn't anoint you to rise up and take it but he gave you a preview of coming attractions to encourage you while you're in your now. To let you know eyes have not seen, ears have not heard all that God has in store for you, but He's given you a preview for the purposes of encouragement, vigilance and spiritual stamina.   1Cor. 2:9

The greatest part of the challenge is to know that you're anointed but not yet appointed but wait patiently until your turn. To have a pastor's anointing and a janitors appointing and still sweep the church, cut the grass; to have a Bishop's anointing and still drive the bus, clean the toilets without complaining.

To see others around you prosper from your word, all the while you remain in a desert place and never be envious, jealous, or mean spirited because it seems like no drops of blessing are falling on you.

Whatever you do, don't loose your self-esteem. Accept the fact and understand that it's not your time yet. You're being processed. What God has for you is for you and He will deliver on time.

As an anointed person of God you must be a good steward of that anointing and protect it at all cost by always exemplifying Christ like character realizing that God is preparing you for a future assignment; something that you can't handle in your now.

The Challenge of Good Ministry

1 Corinthians 2:9-10

*...Eye has not seen, nor ear heard, neither have entered
into the heart of man, the things which god hath
prepared for them that love him.
But God hath revealed them unto us by His Spirit..."*

G od will not always show you pictures or visions of that He is taking you through, but He will show you what he is bringing you to.

Don't be deceived. In order to reach our destiny, and the level of spiritual maturity that is needed for the upcoming task it is mandatory that we are divinely placed and exposed to good ministry. I don't mean just church as usual but ministry of excellence and accuracy. One that requires accountability and your growth is being measured and monitored.

It's also a struggle to be in a good ministry and remain faithful there. There is a great need for more dialog concerning the challenge of being and remaining in a good ministry.

Jesus forewarned his disciples concerning the hardships they would encounter if they became His followers.

Matthew 10: 16-22
16. "Behold I send you forth as sheep in the midst of wolves: be ye therefore wise as serpents and harmless as doves.

*17. But beware of men: for they will deliver you up to the councils,
and they will scourge you in their synagogues;*
*18. And ye shall be brought before governors and kings for my
sake, for a testimony against them and the gentiles.*
*19. But when they deliver you up, take no thought how or what
ye shall speak; for it shall be given you in that same hour what ye
shall speak.*
*20. For it is not you that speak, but the spirit of your father, which
speaketh in you.*
*21. And brother shall deliver up brother to death, and the father
the child: and the children shall rise up against their parents, and
cause them to be put to death.*
*22. And you shall be hated of all men for my name's sake: but he
that endureth to the end shall be saved."*

Jesus doesn't hide the danger or the cost of true discipleship but cautiously calls these words to the remembrance of his followers.

John 16:1-3
1. *"These things have I spoken to you, that you should not be
   offended.*
2. *They shall put you out of the synagogues: yea the time
   cometh, that whosoever killeth you will think that he doeth
   God service.*
3. *And these things will they do unto you, because they have
   not known the father, nor me."*

It's hard. It's tough to be in and stay in a good ministry for you'll surely find yourself on the devil's hit list, especially when you line up with the leadership of the Pastor and the vision of the house.

Coworkers will hate you on your job, because of a good ministry. Your family will ostracize you, friends will despise you and scandalize your name because you finally got in a good ministry, a place of discipline, direction, and destiny. They'll even refer to it as a cult and even a dictatorship. But you know it's far from any of that but it's what God has ordered for your life for such a time as this.

Many folk who were even trying to get you off the street, out of the clubs and in church will despise you, when you're truly delivered and set in a good ministry.

Spiritual warfare will be aimed and waged against you when you're in good ministry pursuing your passion and God's purpose for your life.

The moment you line up and position yourself under a God sent pastor with a vision, for the purposes of committing your unselfish support and encouragement, you come under attack. Especially if you're dedicated to that pastor and ministry and make a declaration to loyally support, with you time talent and treasure.

As you mature and begin to understand the principle of seed time and harvest and you begin to plant seed in good ground, then all hell gets upset because the devil knows the scriptures. You're going to reap what you've sown. If you give, whatever you give. "That" is coming back to you according to Galatians 6:7. And your seed will be returned in a good measure, pressed down, shaken together and running over.   Luke 6:38

Good ministry will challenge you and make you uncomfortable. You feel like running when nobody is chasing you, crying when nothing is wrong. It challenges you to dismiss your pass, face your present fears and pursue your future. It changes your perspective and you begin to apologize when wrong, and submit not only to God but also to delegated authority in your life.

When true ministry reaches your heart it will change your lifestyle, challenge you, stretch you, enlarge you, provokes you to do good, and no matter how good you do it's always ahead of you.

The pastor always preaches over your head; the moment you finally reach one plateau or level of commitment he then say's "let's go higher, you can do more." Good ministry is always in the future. It's progressive, it has a plan for the future and it pushes you into yours.

The Divine Challenge

Ephesians 3:20
Now unto him that is able to do exceeding abundantly
above all that we ask or think, according to the
power that worketh in us...

We often preach and encourage our parishioners by telling them that God will never ask you to do that which you can't do. It's in this stage of my ministry (twenty six years of preaching and 21 years of pastoring) that I personally apologize for that teaching. For now I realize I was wrong.

Our sufficiency is of God and not ourselves...He is able to do exceeding abundantly above all that we ask or think, but according to the power that works in us.

When the call is truly from God it will always challenge you to do what you can't do.

Check out the scripture: Jesus commands a dead man who was dead for 4 days stinking in the grave to get up and come forth.

He challenges a cripple man to pick up his bed and walk;
A blind man to go to the pool and wash;
A lame man to stretch forth his hand
A mortal man to come to him walking on the water
He asks his disciples to feed 20 thousand plus people with 2 fish and 5 biscuits.

All of that seems like a mission impossible. But if you are to grow and mature, that's exactly what you need; a mission that seems impossible.

A divine challenge is identified by a task so awesome that it appears to be a mission impossible. But faith tells you that you can do all things through Christ. (Phil. 4:13)

Just think. How many times you were challenged to do things that you thought you could never do? But look back at your growth that can't be denied; the visible evidence is loving your enemies, praying for those who despitefully use you, tithing, giving offerings, first fruits, sowing seed, paying bills on time even coming to church every Sunday!

Husbands and wives now loving and submitting one to another, birthing new children, starting new businesses, and prospering!

It's strange how a divine challenge will talk to you about where you're going tomorrow while you're upset and discouraged about where you are today.

It will always, challenge you to pursue no matter the circumstances but also promises that you will subdue.

What you see is what you pursue. Sight gives birth to desire. Have you ever been suddenly motivated to go to the refrigerator and eat after seeing a television commercial on food? Of course you have. When you saw a commercial on physical fitness, were you inspired to join a health spa or buy a jogging suit, a treadmill and start walking and jogging? Yes you have.

So God gives us faith pictures called visions. Which show us where we begin and where we end, but never what we will have to endure.

God gives us these photo shots of the future to encourage and inspire us along the way but He only reveals them by His Spirit; So it's extremely important that we continue to develop our relationship with God; fellowship with Him, through meditation and quite time; worship him in Spirit and truth.

Then as we remain in our set place and continue to commune with Him we will receive the right pictures and previews from God our true source; but by all means avoid the wrong photographs the enemy will give us of failure, defeat and discouragement.

NO CHANCE NO ADVANCE-

11 KINGS 7:3-4
*And there were four leprous men at the entering of the gate:
and they said one to another, why sit we here until we die?*

R ecently I was watching the nature channel and my attention was captivated by something intriguing and inter-
esting. They shared some information concerning birds that
reshaped my thoughts as it pertains to this text. It shared how
the same species of birds can have different colors. One can be
multi-colored and the same species can be brown. I learned that
more often than not- the male is colorful and the female is camouflaged (birds). This does not carry over into the genetic breakdown of humans- but there is much for humans to learn from
what happens in the species of some birds.

The colors that the male birds posses serve a threefold purpose. It attracts females—intimidates predators—and scares off
rivals. The female birds who are not multi-colored—in fact are
a muted brown...so that they can fall into the backdrop and
become camouflaged. Purpose: simply because they do not want
to draw attention to their nest and attention to the little ones or
the newborn's they are covering.

Different from birds as human beings—we don't have the
rare opportunity to pick the colors of our feathers but we can
decide whether or not if we're going to be colorful to attract
attention or whether we're going to be muted and just to blend
in to a larger society. Many of us who have decided to be cam-

ouflaged need to understand that camouflage is a metaphor for average. A symbol for the normal, the mundane and the mediocre.

John L. Mason in his book entitled *An Enemy Called Average* says that "a believers' least favorite color should be beige..." Which indicates you would rather remain neutral—never take a side –never take a stand—never make any waves just luke warm and never taking the initiative for anything.

May I remind you that Jesus warns the Church at Laodicea—*"I know thou work—you're neither hot nor cold. I would you were one or the other— seeing that you're not—you're undesirable - I will spurge you out of my mouth"*.

Revelation 3:15-16

When I am hot, I'm colorful and I'm taking a risk that someone is going to see and take note of what I'm doing...(let your light so shine before men...) the most important decision of our lives forces us to come out of camouflage and to put on color. Whenever taking a risk we must move from the safety of invisibility to the threat of being visible. You see high visibility constitutes high vulnerability. And the more visible you become there is more attack on your life from the natural world and the spirit world.

But as long as you hang in the backdrop you are not a threat to yourself...but when visible you will attract more haters — people will lie on you- be jealous and talk about you just because you exhibit more color, character, more personality, and charisma. The camouflaged community will write you off as those who always want to be seen. They're mad, asking why is he getting all the attention? but they don't know that it's something on the inside that will not allow you to fit in with the status quo. You're just too anointed to be anonymous. As a consequence you don't want to dress like everybody else, drive what everybody else is driving. There's something innately about you that says "I'm about risky business".

The greater the opportunity, the greater the risk that's required for success. We are familiar with the teachings of

Jesus. "*...For unto whom much is given, of him shall much be required*"... Luke 12:48

But today I also want to suggest to you that if you have a great gift you will also be challenged with great risk. If you do not want to risk anything great then you're not going anywhere great; but there are a sundered number of people who have resolved in their lives today...I've got nothing to lose. And because I've got nothing to loose —I'm going to take a big chance to make my advance. I insist on taking a risk to get what God has for me.

It was Dr. Mike Murdock of the wisdom center in Denton TX, who said "if you want something you never had—you must do something you've never done". You cannot expect an over-flow and continue doing the same old thing by keeping the same old routine.

Seriously, on a personal note I'm tired of hearing the New Years clichés that believers declare each year. Such as "In 01 I'm the one, In—02—God has much for you, In 03-shout for Jubilee-04—Come back for more— In 05 We'll really thrive—In 08 were going get straight"... In 09 we're coming from behind; in 2010 we're destined to win"... but be careful to observe many are still doing the same thing and haven't experienced any increase or the slightest breakthrough.

It's time to do something different. I dare you to take a risk. In 2010 you can't afford to assemble yourselves around *safe* people but look to connect with *faith* people. Because when I walk by faith it's not always safe. I don't know if or when I'll fail or succeed...but I'm going take a risk. I'm going to take a chance toward my advance. Yes, I must put my best foot for-ward, and do the best I can to succeed. I must remember the slogan; to get something I never had, I must do something I've never done. In 09 I'll come from behind—in 2010 I will win because I insist on taking risk! I will take a chance toward my advance"...*The kingdom suffers violence and the violent—take it by force*... Matt. 11:12

Excuse Yourself

The reason you must excuse yourself from the company of safe people is because safe people don't want to take risk. Truth is they're captivated by fear because risk is connected to failure... and the fear of failure has the potential to fossilize.

Many fail to see that failure is necessary for success, it enables you to overcome fear and activate faith...Any person has who has never failed has never taken a risk—and probably has never succeeded. But every time you try something new you risk failure, embarrassment, and shame; but at least you can say "I tried to do something". While many are sitting back fault-finding, those who truly want to succeed look for opportunities thru risk.

John C. Maxwell says in his book *FAILING FORWARD* that *"the difference between average people and achieving people is their perception of and response to failure"*.

You must understand that often time opportunity is hidden within opposition. So when you fail to risk because of opposition you close the door of opportunity. Everyday I am forced to risk an aspect of my character. Each day there is a situation that pulls me into a risk.

Everyone wants to be loved. But if you've been in love before you know that's risky.

Many today avoid a close relationship for they've been in love before and got played like a banjo, got hurt, run over, hood-winked-used and abused.

Because of this foul treatment you received from someone who didn't respect or value you, your resolve is to never trust another.

Then when you really receive a decent proposal your attitude may be: "you're asking me to spend my life with you? I must admit that you are very attractive and all but a life time commitment? I don't think so. That's risky business...

Bishop you're asking me to come to church and sit here for 2-3hrs. Looking all cool, calm, and collected while my life is falling apart? I've got to work 24-7 to keep the bills paid, lights and power on –food on the table, house note, car note and cable bill paid. I don't have time for all that emotionalism I must spend my time and energy where it counts. But God is saying to you in 2010, "it is risky business to never enter into my presence; and it more risky to enter into my presence and ignore me, fail to reverence me." You must do something to realize, recognize, and acknowledge that the Lord is in His Holy temple. Let everything that has breath, Praise the Lord!

So God says each time you enter into my presence I want you to take a risk but a calculated risk—one that's base on promise and expectation.

The promise is: The Lord will make a way somehow—He will open the windows of heaven and bless me with an abundance—my God will supply all of my needs according to His riches in glory through Christ Jesus

The expectation is:

I don't know when-where or how but if he said it He'll do it, if he spoke it He'll bring it to pass. When my praises go up I expect His blessings comes down. He's an on time God, yes He is.

I know he can—I know he will—but if not....In other words in 08—if all you did was raise your hand—this year clap—last you just rocked side to side— this year—get up out of your seat—last year you just stood—this year you've gotta stomp—If last year you stomped—this year you gotta jump—last year you ran—this year you've got to dance...last year you just gave—this year you must Tithe—last year you Tithed –this year you must sow.. You must take a risk and say I want something I never had, so this year I'm going to take a risk and do something I never done before.

In his book "Seizing Your Divine Moment"*Erwin McManis*—states that "there is a space in life between once upon a time and happy ever after. In between once upon a time and happy ever after is where the risk comes in...But most saints –delusional –want once upon a time and happy ever after without any risk.

Listen, whenever God puts an anointing on you and an appointment in your life. He will make you risk something and from other peoples perspective you will look crazy.

Can you imagine the fear and risk that went along with the assignment of getting into a fiery furnace heated 7 times hotter than normal? Can you imagine-the fear and risk that went along with getting into a den of lions without a sword or even a stick or staff? It takes faith and risk. Risk is= motivation after information for formation...The only way that you take a risk is that you have gathered some information. You have to ask yourself the question "what is this going to cost me if I open this business—acknowledge this call on my life—walk the aisle and say I will, until death do us part. What's the cost for me to leave this secure job with benefits to go back to school for my degree—to walk away from a marriage or relationship that I'm miserable in And God can't get any glory from?

What is it going to cost me when God has put a premium over my head?" So before you take the risk, gather the information. There is an oxy-moronic phrase called "fail safe". This means –there is no way for it not to work.

God says get all the information that says and shows it can't work. You're not taking a risk until you have enough people to tell you it can't happen.

When folk say you can't do it—it' will never work out or you're not qualified—that's when you take a bonified risk and say—I'm gonna show them. God said that in 2009 victory is mine. In 2010 I shall win. For this is the year he's gonna shut the haters up. Everything that they said you couldn't do, you couldn't have, he's going to bring it to pass...but only if you're willing to take a risk.

In 2nd Kings 7 here we have four men with leprosy—leprosy in biblical time is equivalent to HIV today—there is no human cure—it works in ones blood stream- shuts down your immune system and make you vulnerable to all types of disease. They're not supposed to be in the city and they have been assigned to a community called a leper's camp. Outside of the city and no one knows how to handle their disease. It's a time of famine, they're hungry and diseased and about to die. They've been sitting outside of gate for some time... No doctors came, no immunizations shots—no meals on wheels—no outreach team—no missionaries or serve shelter—no health care available to help them—They sat at the gate all year. They begin to evaluate their situation and unanimously agreed among themselves "that it's a brand new year and it's time to do something different—we've been in this situation now for a year I'm sick of waiting on help—.

In order get something we've never had –we've got to do something we've never done."

I don't know who I may be addressing but there's someone reading this book who's sick and tired of waiting on somebody else to help them; Somebody else to pay their rent, somebody else to provide them transportation, someone else to pay their bills, somebody to take them out.

This year I'm going risk making myself happy. This year I'm going to do something for me that nobody else would do.

Single saints: Sometimes you got to do like Alicia Keys as she says to Mos Def: I don't normally do this(secular song) –call a man but—and you don't even know my name— but something inside says take a risk to talk to you- after work...maybe we can sit down and over a soda or a cup of coffee work something out!

Someone is reading this now asking what do I have to lose? In 03—we were broke—04 busted- 05-disgusted—06 fell for the devil's tricks—07 was far from heaven-08 we didn't get it straight, 09 we're still behind, 010 we're want to win, so what do we have to lose? It's a brand new year let's take a chance to make an advance.

The leper's attitude was if we stay here we're going to die; we might as well try it and see what we come up with... It can't be any worse than what we're stuck with right now...Why sit here and do nothing?

I am challenging you to ask yourself, your spouse, your friend, how long are you going sit here and do nothing about your situation? How long are you going stay depressed and send out invitations to your pity party? Wait for them to call you back—wait for somebody to ask you out—wait for somebody to make you feel special? How long? You ought to make a bold declaration and say "Not another day! I'm going do it if I have to do it by myself...

So this year to make an advance you must take a chance, a risk doing something that's not so safe...Try something challenging that you might fail at but at least you can say that you tried.

Listen. Time is winding up, and none of us are getting any younger. This year get up from sitting on the couch feeling sorry for yourself and depressed about your situation...*Lift up your heads, O ye gates; and be ye lifted up, ye everlasting doors; and the King of glory shall come in.* Psalm 24:7

Please note there are lepers at church. You may be acquainted with a few who sit in church and sit in church—and they sit in church come late and sit in church- leave early and sit in church-

Maybe just once or twice a month but just sit in church- don't Tithe but sit up in the church—complaining about everything, at what others are wearing-but sitting up in the church. Some just left the club dancing—but sitting up in the church— had a wild party at home last night –but sitting up in the church talking about the saints who are trying- but sitting up in the church. Laughing at the saints shout and rejoice but they only sit in Church.

But God said these are they who will not experience the breakthrough or the overflow...but I'm looking for the saints who can't sit down...the folks who risk giving me a crazy praise right in the middle of it. The folk who said like Jeremiah "it feels like fire..."

The Paradox of the Election Principle

1 Samuel 16:13
Then Samuel took the horn of oil, and anointed him
in the midst of his brethren; and the spirit of the Lord
came upon David from that day forward...

D on't miss this very important principle. The election principal has a ministry of it's own. A good ministry that will
bring the shall be's into their now.

It will give you something now that you can't use until then;
but you must have it, and hold it, never use it, and never loose it.

Let me explain further.

The ministry of the election principal came to the house of
Jesse looking for a King among a bunch of farmers. It had oil
that wouldn't flow until it found the right head. Many got into
position but they couldn't get the power. The oil just wouldn't
flow.

It asked for the elected son and reaches around a line of
others and picks out the least likely, the rejected one. God gets
the person that's not groomed, least prepared; the one everybody has their foot on.

David was brought from the pasture to the palace. He didn't
have clothes, statue, reputation, grooming or mentoring. He was
without possessions or position, didn't know protocol or politics.
But he did have praise, promise and much potential.

Likewise, God wants to promote you today. Even if you
haven't been trained or prepared, have no seniority or degree.

Others may be better equipped and qualified but remember when God sent Samuel to Jesse' house to anoint His chosen King of Israel he gave him explicit instructions; But the LORD said unto Samuel, Look not on his countenance, or on the height of his stature; because I have refused him: for the LORD seeth not as man seeth; for man looketh on the outward appearance, but the LORD looketh on the heart. (1 King 16:7)

Therefore many people in this season who don't look the part will be chosen

for you have a heart for the things of God, and have been pre-elected for His divine purposes.

Remember, *all things work together for the good of those who love God, to those who are called, according to His purposes.* (Rom. 8:28.)

The Search for F.A.T.T. Folk

God is looking for F.A.T.T. people. Don't misunderstand me. When I use the word F.A.T.T. please note that I am referring to an acronym F. A. T. T.

F—Faithful *It is required of steward that a man be found Faithful 1 cor. 4:2*

The Marines may be looking for a few good men but God is looking for a few faithful ones.

In today's world, commitment, dependability, and trust-worthiness are traits that are hard to come by. Yet, God longs for His children to be faithful to His call on their lives. II Chronicles 16:9 says, "For the eyes of the Lord range throughout the earth to strengthen those whose hearts are fully committed to Him." Thus, God is eager to bless those who are sold out to following His plan for their lives.

In Proverbs 28:20, Solomon wrote, "A faithful man will be richly blessed." And that same theme is echoed in Proverbs 3:3-4 "[that if] love and faithfulness never leave you . . . you will win favor and a good name in the sight of God and man."

Being faithful to serve God and to keep Him as your first priority in every area of your life is crucial to realizing the purpose God has in creating you and in fulfilling the destiny He has designed for you. The Bible is full of examples of men and women whose unfaithfulness to the Lord cost them their lives as well the blessings that could have been theirs. Saul, the first king of Israel was once a powerful and wealthy leader, but he caved in to his selfishness and his desire to exalt himself and later committed suicide. The closing caption over Saul's life in I Chronicles 10:13 reads "Saul died because he was unfaithful to the Lord . . . "A tragic end to a life brimming with so much potential in the beginning. Proverbs 14:12 reiterates this truth by saying that "There is a way that seems right to a man, but in the end it leads to death."

Just as faithfulness holds immeasurable blessings from the hand of God, unfaithfulness to God and His Word only lead us to hopelessness and eventual destruction. Walking in God's will is the only path that ultimately brings any lasting rewards. The world's ways offer temporary fixes at best and destructive ends at worst. Being faithful in a faithless world is not always easy in the short-term but it is always better in the long-run. Psalms 15:4-5 states that the man "who keeps his oath even when it hurts . . . will never be shaken. Ask God to make you a faithful servant today so that you too can withstand the storms of life and remain anchored on the ever-faithful God who cannot be moved.

<u>A — Available</u> *Brethren, look out among you seven men of good report we may appoint over this business Acts 6: 3*

God's opinion of us does matter! How God chooses to use us, can affect eternity!

Psalm 51:11-13-Cast me not away from thy presence; and take not thy holy spirit from me. Restore unto me the joy thy salvation; and uphold me with thy free spirit. Then will I teach transgressors thy ways and sinners shall be converted unto thee.

David realized that because of the sin that he allowed in his life God wasn't using him. The same is true for us today. If we allow sin into our lives, if we don't make ourselves available to God we are going to be left standing on the side lines.

I'm thankful that God doesn't use the same criteria for choosing what Christians He uses that third graders use for picking their team mates. But we still need to make ourselves available to Him.

Will God choose us? Or will we be left standing on the sidelines?

Let's look at 3 Criteria for making ourselves available to God. Three Criteria that Saul lost that lead to God rejecting him.

Lost his Humble Spirit-

One of the main reasons God choose Saul to be king in the first place was the fact that he was humble. He was little in his own eyes. But Saul lost his humble spirit.

If we are going to make ourselves available, we must eliminate pride from our lives.

Proverbs 6:16-17 These six things doth the LORD hate: yea, seven are an abomination unto him: A proud look

Proverbs 16:18-Pride goeth before destruction, and an haughty spirit before a fall.

Proverbs 16: 19-Better it is to be of an humble spirit with the lowly, than to divide the spoil with the proud.

"God made the world out of nothing, and it is only when we become nothing He can make something out of us". -Martin Luther

But how is it that we are to maintain a humble spirit? Let's look at two examples of a humble spirit. The first example is a Spirit of Service.

> *-Let this mind be in you, which was also in Christ Jesus: Who, being in the form of God, thought it not robbery to be equal with God: But made himself of no reputation, and took upon himself the form of a servant, and was made in the likeness of men: And being found in fashion as a man, he humbled himself, and became obedient unto death, even the death of the Cross. Philippians 2:5-8*

Self-righteous service comes through human effort. True service comes from a relationship with the divine Other deep inside.

Self-righteous service is impressed with the "big deal." True service finds it almost impossible to distinguish the small from the large service.

Self-righteous service requires external rewards. True service rests contented in hiddenness.

Self-righteous service is highly concerned about results. True service is free of the need to calculate results.

Self-righteous service picks and chooses whom to serve. True service is indiscriminate in its ministry.

Self-righteous service is affected by moods and whims. True service ministers simply and faithfully because there is a need.

Self-righteous service is temporary. True service is a life-style.

Self-righteous service is without sensitivity. It insists on meeting the need even when to do so would be destructive. True service can withhold the service as freely as perform it.

Self-righteous service fractures community. True service, on the other hand, builds community.

Here are several signs of a serving spirit...

<u>Will serve anywhere in ministry</u>

Philippians 2:7-But made himself of no reputation...

<u>Transition well in ministry</u>

<u>Don't need to get the credit-Goal is to please God not others</u>

For do I now persuade men, or God? or do I seek to please men? for if I yet pleased men, I should not be the servant of Christ.
Galatians 1:10-

-And whatsoever ye do, do it heartily, as to the Lord, and not unto men
Colossians 3:23

<u>Puts others before self</u>

A new commandment I give unto you, That ye love one another; as I have loved you, that ye may also love one another. By this shall all men know that ye are my disciples, if ye love one another.
John 13:34-35-

If we are going to make ourselves available to God by having a spirit of humility, we must have a spirit of service, not only a spirit of service but a Spirit of Meekness.

Meekness isn't weakness, it is really strength under God's control.

Let's look at several signs of a meek spirit...

<u>Does not have to have the last word</u>
Does not have to always be heard

-Wherefore, my beloved brethren, let every man be swift to hear, slow to speak, slow to wrath:

James 1:19

-In the multitude of words there wanteth not sin, but he that refraineth his lips is wise.

Proverbs 10:19

Does not have to always be right
-Only by pride cometh contention (contention means debate) *but with the well advised is wisdom- Proverbs 13:10.*

Does not have to always be in charge
Does not perform brash actions
So we can see that we must maintain a humble spirit! Saul lost his humble spirit

Lost his Obedient Spirit-vs. 19-23

Saul was given a clear command by God and he disobeyed! It is imperative, if we are going to make ourselves available to God, that we maintain an obedient spirit towards the Word of God

V22-to obey is better than sacrifice
V23-Rebellion is as the sin of witchcraft, and stubbornness is
as iniquity and idolatry

What idol are you worshiping? God takes disobedience very seriously. So seriously that he puts it on the same level as idol worship. He calls our rebellion witchcraft. In verse number 23 Samuel very bluntly tells King Saul *Thou hast rejected the Word of the LORD!*

What in this book are you rejecting?

Throughout the New Testament we are given five baseline characteristics of a good Christian.

We must do our Devotions.

James 4:8-Draw nigh to God, and he will draw night to you.
"Rose early to seek God, and found Him whom my soul
loveth. Who would not rise early to meet such company?"
Robert Murrary MCheyne

"Complacency is a deadly foe of all spiritual growth..He
waits to be wanted." "Call unto Me.." A.W. Tozer

We must be obedient in our Prayers.
-Men ought always to pray   Luke 18:1
How's our prayer life? -
Every Christian, throughout the Bible and throughout
history who has made himself available to God,
have been Christians who know to pray.
"The little value we place on prayer is proven
by the little time we spend praying."
"Satan trembles when he sees the weakest saint
upon his knees."-William Cowper

We obey through our devotion to Him
We obey through our prayers to Him

We obey through our Church Attendance
-Not forsaking the assembling of ourselves together, as the manner
of some is; but exhorting one another: and so much the more, as
ye see the day approaching.

Hebrews 10:25

I think we would all agree that day is approaching and fast!
If we want God to use us we must be in our local church! It is

God's ordained institution for reaching the world. God has no mavericks who are just out there doing their own thing. We will not be used by God if we are not being faithful to His church. Do you want to make yourself available to God? Be in church!

<u>We must be obedient in our Tithing.</u>
Really what it all boils down to is giving ourselves to God.

> *And this they did, not as we had hoped, but first gave their own selves to the Lord, and unto us by the will of God*
> *2 Corinthians 8:5-.*

J.L. Kraft, head of the Kraft Cheese Corporation, who had given approximately 25% of his enormous income to Christian causes for many years, said, "The only investment I ever made which has paid consistently increasing dividends is the money I have given to the Lord."

When you study the churches in the New Testament that were on fire for God, you will find that they were all giving churches. The churches at Macedonia, the Church at Philippi, the Churches at Thessalonica, all churches who God had 100% of including their finances.

Last, we make ourselves available to God by being obedient in the area of Evangelism.

> *-And Jesus came and spake unto them, saying, All power is given unto me in heaven and in earth. Go ye therefore, and teach all nations, baptizing them in the name of the Father, and of the Son, and of the Holy Ghost: Teaching them to observe all things whatsoever I have commanded you: and, lo, I am with you alway, even unto the end of the world. Amen.*
> *Matthew 28:18-20*

God has given us a command to tell others about Him. How affective are we in telling others about Him?

We make ourselves available to God by being obedient to Him!

Saul lost his humble spirit
Saul lost his obedient spirit

Lost the Spirit of God on his life-vs. 26-28

There is nothing that you or I can do, without the power of God in our lives.

John 15:5-without me ye can do nothing

How can I be filled with the Holy Spirit? Can I loose the Holy Spirit? First of all lets look at the definition of being filled with the Holy Spirit. We are going to define being filled with the Holy Spirit, as opposed to being indwelt with the Holy Spirit.
Indwelling of the Holy Spirit-This happens at the moment of salvation. When we got saved, the Holy Spirit took up residence in our lives.

1 Corinthians 3:16-Know ye not that ye are the temple of God, and that the Spirit of God dwelleth in you?

Now the Christians at Corinth did not model being available for God's use, however they still had the Holy Spirit living inside of them.
We can never loose the Holy Spirit. We are permanently indwelt with Him.

Ephesians 4:30-And grieve not the holy Spirit of God, whereby ye are sealed unto the day of redemption.

According to John 14-16 when Jesus left this earth He left us with His Holy Spirit in order to replace His physical absence on earth. And until the day of redemption, when we are once again in His physical presence we will be sealed with the Holy Spirit.
Next lets look at the <u>Filling of the Holy Spirit.</u>

Ephesians 5:18-And be not drunk with wine, wherein is excess; but be filled with the Spirit.

So, if I, as a Christian, am permanently indwelt with the Holy Spirit, why do I need to be filled with the Holy Spirit? Being filled with the Holy Spirit is a choice I make to yield my life to His control.

Now that we have defined being filled with the Holy Spirit, let us **Understand being filled with the Holy Spirit.**

First of all, <u>it is a daily choice I must make.</u>

1 Corinthians 15:31-I die daily

If I am going to make myself available to God, every day I must decide to be filled with the Holy Spirit. To present my body a living sacrifice to God.

Prayer:

> "God, today I want to be filled with your Spirit. I want to do, only what will please You. I want to live in such a manner that will bring glory to Your name. God I present my body totally to Your control, do with it as You wish."

<u>**I must also be aware of His presence.**</u>

Know ye not that ye are the temple of God, and that the Spirit of God dwelleth in you? 1 Corinthians 3:16-

Really in this verse Paul is rebuking the Corinthians for not living as though God was with them everywhere they went, because He was! And He is with us every minute of every day! The key to constantly yielding my life to Him, is really being aware that He is there!

When we as Christians are aware of His presence we are making ourselves available to Him to use.

We must also understand that We can grieve the Holy Spirit.

And grieve not the holy Spirit of God, whereby ye are sealed unto the day of redemption. Ephesians 4:30-

I will always be my fathers son. There is nothing I can do to change that. But I can grieve him and loose fellowship with him. The same is true with the Holy Spirit. I cannot loose Him, but I can grieve Him, and strain that relationship, and when I do, I am no longer making myself available to God.

We have viewed three criteria for making myself available to God.

Feeding of the five thousand-would not have happened if a small boy had not made himself available to God.

Calvary, would not have happened is Jesus had made Himself available.

Pentecost, would not have happened if Peter and the others had not made themselves available to God.

All the churches that were planted throughout the New Testament, would not have happened if the Church at Antioch and Paul and his team weren't available.

What will it be? Will you make yourself available? Or will you just sit and watch from the side?

You know at the end of 1 Samuel 15 God repented that He had ever made Saul King. Will God change His mind about you? Or will you make yourself available?

T—Teachable *Take my yoke upon you and learn of me Matt. 11-29*
A Teachable Spirit

A Teachable Spirit

Why do some people learn and others don't? Why are some people easy to teach and others aren't? Is it intelligence? Education? Heredity? In looking back on over 35 years of teaching, I believe that a "teachable spirit" is the one quality needed.

1. The hearer has more effect on how much is received than the teacher. In the parable of the sower, the same sower sowed the same seed on the four different types of ground. In other words, the same teacher, or preacher, with the same techniques presented the same message. The condition of the ground made the difference in results. The good ground (those with a teachable spirit) brought forth many-fold. I recall a time when I had the privilege to minister in a church in Brazil that was so crowded that after the preaching people had to take turns to come to the altar. Why such a tremendous response compared to when I have preached in the United States? The difference was the hunger and thirst for the word. In other words, they had a teachable spirit.

2. A person who comes with an attitude that they already know as much as the teacher can't be taught. "The full soul loatheth an honeycomb; but to the hungry soul every bitter thing is sweet:" (Proverbs 27:7). There are some saints and ministers that will never come to a seminar unless they are asked to teach. They think they already know all they need to know. But the hungry soul, the one with the teachable spirit, will be filled.

3. Some have the attitude that they have no need for a man to teach them for they think they get it all straight from God. It is true that the Holy Ghost can teach you things that no man can teach you, however, if this was all that was needed, then why would God have given teachers to the church? Teachers were

given "for the perfecting of the saints, for the work of the ministry, for the edifying of the body of Christ." (Eph. 4:11)

4. The way a person receives teaching tells something about his character and will eventually determine his destiny. "Reprove not a scorner, lest he hate thee: rebuke a wise man, and he will love thee. Give instruction to a wise man and he will yet be wiser: teach a just man, and he will increase in learning." "Correction is grievous unto him that forsaketh the way: and he that hateth reproof shall die." A wise man has a teachable spirit and gets wiser while the one who is not teachable will eventually lose out.

There are many examples of teachable people in the Bible. David said, "Shew me thy ways, O Lord and teach me thy paths. Lead me in thy truth and teach me..." When Ezra read the law of Moses "from morning to noon, the ears of all the people were attentive...." The scripture seems to indicate that the people stood during all this time. The disciples had a teachable spirit when they asked Jesus, "Teach us to pray." On the day of Pentecost people "gladly received the word and three thousand were added." After Cornelius told Peter his vision he said, "Now therefore are we all here present before God, to hear all the things that are commanded thee of God." And when Peter spoke, the Holy Ghost fell on those that heard the word because they were teachable. Paul called those at Berea noble because they received the word with all readiness of mind."

I have heard the setting of the sail on a sailboat is called the "attitude" of the sail. The same wind can cause a sailboat to go in different directions. It is the attitude of a teachable spirit that will enable us to go in a right direction.

The old song, "Tell Me The Story Of Jesus" includes this line which describes the teachable spirit, "Those who know it best seem hungering and thirsting to hear it like the rest." No matter what our age, let us pray, "God give me a teachable spirit."

T—Trustworthy Servants must be grave not double tongued 1 Tim. 3:8

How often do you use the word "trust" or "trustworthy" in everyday conversation? It's really rather uncomplicated, isn't it? I have a friend who often punctuates a comment he makes by lifting his hand in the oath position and saying, *"Trust me!"* But using this phrase feels even more significant when you confess: "I am trustworthy and faithful as a person and as a minister in my relationship and service to others!" What if each one of us could make such a worthy confession?

Contemporary Uses: To be trustworthy is a core quality within a person, to be worthy of trust, what you really are down on the inside of you. Flip Wilson's *"What you see is what you get"* may be what you say about yourself to others as they take a view from the outside. But *"What you get is who I really am"* is the inside reality others most often look for. What does it mean? Others can rely on your actions to be helpful and not harmful. You use power and authority in a way that respects others, their rights, feelings, ideas, and possessions. You practice your belief in the God you confess to serve, and you believe in yourself as His servant. Other such descriptive behavior patterns and actions of trust-building are included throughout this chapter.

Glossary: When you think of the terms used for trustworthy, or trustworthiness, it may enrich an initial understanding; words such as: faithful, integrity, dependability, reliable, truthful, responsible, honorable, and principled. Dictionaries further report:

- trustworthy: 1—worthy of trust or belief; "a trustworthy report"; "an experienced and trustworthy traveling companion [syn.: trusty] [ant: untrustworthy].
- 2—taking responsibility for one's conduct and obligations; "trustworthy public servants" (WordNet® 1.6, ©1997 Princeton University).

- trust: 1—assured reliance on the character, ability, strength, or truth of someone or something;
- 2—dependence on something future or contingent: HOPE;
- 3—a charge or duty imposed in faith or confidence or as a condition of some relationship. (<u>Merriam-Webster's Collegiate Dictionary</u>)

Scripture Teaching About Trustworthiness

To examine and to develop our lives for trustworthy life and leadership we place priority on the biblical witness. In the New Testament, there is a family of Greek words that clearly and extensively carry the meaning *"to trust, trusting, and trustworthy"*:

- *"pisteuo"* - *to believe, to trust, to have faith, to have confidence*
- *"pistis"* - *faithfulness, reliability; or, trust, confidence, faith*
- *"pistos"* - *trustworthy, faithful, dependable, inspiring trust or faith*
- *"pistoõ"* - *to show oneself faithful, trustworthy; to prove oneself trustworthy; to feel confidence, to be convinced*

A selection of texts illustrates how these terms are used:

- 1 Cor. 1:9 and 10:13 - *"God alone is worthy of complete trust; He is entirely trustworthy in all His dealings with us and in bringing us into fellowship through Christ."* (**NIV**)
- Hebrews 2:17 - *"Christ, unlike human priests, was a faithful, reliable high priest."* (NIV)
- Romans 10:8-10 - *"'Faith' or 'trust' in Christ is the connecting experience between people and the Lord's salvation."* (**NIV**)
- Heb. 3:5 - *"Moses was faithful, trustworthy in all things in his house."* (NIV)
- 1 Cor. 7:25 - *"Paul's claim to be trustworthy was his basis to claim to be heard."* (NIV)

ORDINARY PEOPLE/ EXTRAORDINARY THINGS

ACTS 14:15
...Sirs why do ye these things? We are also men
of like passions as you...

A word of prophecy: God desires to do extra-ordinary things. He's an incredible God who exists to do extra-ordinary things in earth as it is in heaven but He chooses to use ordinary people.

The Prophet Daniel in Ch. 11: 32 prophesies that the people that know their God shall be strong and do mighty exploits— — extra-ordinary things. Jesus in a prophetical statement says in John 14:12 "verily, verily, I say unto you, he that believeth on me, the works that I do shall he do also; and greater works than these shall he do because I go unto my father. Vs. 13 and whatsoever ye shall ask in my name, that will I do, that the Father may be glorified in the Son. Vs. 14 if ye shall ask any thing in my name, I will do it."

The kingdom of heaven is at hand and it's about to manifest itself on earth but be it unto you according to your faith.

We must understand and appreciate how significant it is to have radical faith in this season. It doesn't matter what Daniel says—Jesus says—I say –until you believe it. As a man thinketh so is he. So I believe that there are some ordinary believers today who attend Church each and every Sunday not just for church as usual... But who are there believing God for the extra-ordinary things in their life.

If I was only expecting ordinary things I wouldn't go to church...I don't need God or the church to live an ordinary life if everything that I hope to have out of this life is the same things that everyone else has in the world. I don't need this. So what motivates me is my belief in the extra-ordinary—supernatural—beyond human reasoning... That drives me out to the House of God... to seek His favor...to learn more of Him and His word. To discover what He has in store for me according to his precious promises...You see- for many of us this more than just a saving station... it's a feeding station... a harvest assembly...I've been planting...sowing...hoping...dreaming...and this place is where my faith is feed to believe that something extra-ordinary is going to happen... if I come to reap the harvest God has promise me...empower myself with vision and discernment that I might take back what the devil stole from me when I didn't know any better.

The world can have the ordinary but I came for something extra-ordinary...not just for life but life more abundantly...Not quantity but quality out of this life—I want all that God has for me...I don't only want more—I want it all. Not pie in the sky in the bye and bye but God desires for the saints to rule, reign, and have dominion in the here and now.

There are a few things in this text I feel are incredibly important I want to share. I think God is saying to you.

In order to experience more than the average most people need an extra-ordinary challenge. As Paul and Barnabas were ministering in Lystra—They encounter a lame man—impotent in his feet—incapacitated. In his feet he cannot walk. If you do extra-ordinary things- you need someone with extra-ordinary insight.

Paul perceived (discernment—extra-ordinary insight) not only was the man cripple but he had never walked. In order to be effective in ministry we need extraordinary discernment. You must know what you're ministering to and or what infirmity or spirit you're facing. Without this supernatural insight we may sometimes find ourselves prescribing the wrong remedy for the wrong symptom.

It took something not only from Paul but also from the lame man.... Vs. 9 says—the cripple man heard Paul speak... well the question remains what was Paul preaching. I submit to you he was preaching the Gospel...the whole package—salvation—healing and deliverance. Some folk believe if I look sorry enough –and life looks bad enough then God feels sorry for you and just heals you and delivers you out of your troubles by his vast reservoir of mercy... not so.

The reality is, the just shall live by faith...Paul caught up in one of the most powerful but yet revelatory doxologies in Eph. 3: 20 says now unto him who is able to do exceeding abundantly above all that we ask or think, according to the power that worketh in us...We as believers have to move from faith to faith. Progressively coming—hearing—believing... doing... by radical faith.

Faith like water seeks it's own level—the deep calls unto the deep...grace can't help itself but looks to help someone who needs it...wants it...

In Vs. 10 Paul said with a loud voice exercising extra-ordinary boldness to speak... command the blessing...healing and deliverance... He saw faith in the man. Although his feet were lame and his legs didn't cooperate with his nervous system...it didn't affect his hearing and his ability to believe. But there's where good preaching and teaching ministry will prove itself... it will commanded you to do something that your circumstances say you cannot do...Real good ministry will challenge you to do something extraordinary. Paul looked at him without being polite or apologetic and commanded him to get up.

Vs. 11. Now when the people saw it...these secular heathens—what Paul had done—how he spoke to this lame man and wrought this extra-ordinary miracle—they were perplexed... and said these men are gods...and come down to us in the likeness of men... They began to liken them unto gods...we live in a society that likes to make gods out of people. Now we should give honor where it is due but not deify people. We make gods out of people for some of the craziest reasons…a little girl wins a talent contest –yes she can sing and has a record deal…but now she becomes an unqualified role model.

Some little joker in the hood who learns how to run –running from the police officers… now he gets on the football field and runs…now we say you ought to speak to your generation because you can run…Gospel singers make a hit record…now he's pastor…Just because you can sing doesn't mean you have a call or anointing to shepherd a flock.

We love to make heroes and deify people and then we destroy them…. people set you up and then watch you fall.

They will nickname you…and bring sacrifices unto you… so Paul and Barnabas get word of it…they rush down to the people—rent their clothes and said no!!! You will not make gods of us…they knew that the people would soon discover that they were human and kill them. As it was then so it is today. Please catch this all you talented and gifted people. Paul said we are not gods but are men of like passions. Although he did extraordinary feats he insisted on being an ordinary person. You see the greatest miracle is not that the lame man was healed but that God used an ordinary person to do it…

It's so important …because when the people around you think that you are so super special it gives them a license to do nothing; not to even try, but they cast their expectancy upon you.

But when the chosen people that God is using would only say, "It's not me but the God in me. I'm just like you, and if God uses me…he will use you too… you can do this."

No matter how God operates in your life never loose your ordinary-ness… Because God gets the glory when you remain ordinary…God strength is made perfect in your weakness. Yes God is going to use me…not because I'm special but because He is an extra-ordinary God!! Paul says we are men of like passions –just like you…

As you operate under this extraordinary anointing Vs. 19 you will come under extra-ordinary attack. If you are going to be used of God to do extra-ordinary things expect "ordinary attack..." these men came not to just stop Paul but they came to kill him... not because you are ordinary but because you are doing extra-ordinary things. They didn't try and hang him, thrust him through with the sword, Shoot him with an arrow ...but they desired to stone him to death. There are many people today who are experiencing extra-ordinary attacks. Finances... family...relationship...you see stones come slowly... one after another as you strive to do the will of God. But be encouraged when you come under attack for it is then for qualify for extra-ordinary deliverance.

Vs. 19 they stoned Paul supposing him to be dead. Sometimes life will knock you out cold and the enemy will assume you to be dead. They start planning your funeral—whose going to get his car...his house, his clothes... dividing up the possessions; but as my grandmother used to tell "me every closed eye ain't sleep... every goodbye ain't gone".....After the stoning and pronunciation of his death, it's then that extraordinary deliverance took place. The disciples stood round about Paul and he recovered, rose up and came back into the city.

Saints be encouraged after they persecute you, and leave you for dead; get ready for a miraculous comeback with extra-ordinary deliverance.

The next day Paul and Barnabas traveled into the neighboring city of Der'be continued to preach the gospel to that city and taught many and exhorting them to continue in the faith; for we all must through *much tribulation* enter into the Kingdom of God.

The Anointing

Luke 4:18-19
18 The Spirit of the Lord is upon me, because he hath
anointed me to preach the gospel to the poor; he hath sent
me to heal the brokenhearted, to preach deliverance to the
captives, and recovering of sight to the blind, to set at liberty
them that are bruised,
19 To preach the acceptable year of the Lord.

"Anointing", not just a powerful word but a supernatural/powerful thing in the Old and New Testaments; but yet not many believers today have a clear understanding of it. Yes even though we call our Lord "Christ" which means "anointed one" very few Christians today believe this word has any direct bearing on his or her personal life.

The ancient use of the word anoint simply meant to rub in, pour or smear on oil. Quiet often it was oil with a fragrance. The Old Testament use of this word among God's people signified a transfer of authority, power and honor. By pouring oil upon God's priests or His chosen kings, these individuals became spiritually empowered to conduct the business of that office; Therefore the "term" anointed came to mean a person chosen for a special commission, but totally dependent on God and His plans.

In Luke 4:18-19 Jesus began His public ministry and announced His calling publicly. He stated that he had been anointed by the Spirit to do a number of things:

1. To preach the gospel to the poor
2. To heal the brokenhearted
3. To preach deliverance to the captives
4. To recover sight to the blind
5. To liberate the bruised
6. To preach the acceptable year of the Lord

Please note the anointing is given to do; to actively engage in a God given enterprise and not just to sit, wear, and possess without purpose or an assignment.

We also note before Jesus sent out His twelve disciples to minister, Matthew records that:

He called them unto Himself and gave them power (anointed/ordained) over unclean spirits, to cast them out, and to heal all manner of disease. (Matt.10:1)

Mark records that:
...They cast out many devils, and anointed with oil many that were sick, and healed them (Mark 6:13)

The practice of anointing was definitely a major part of the early Church's ministry.

Is any sick among you? let him call for the elders of the church; and let them pray over him, anointing him with oil in the name of the Lord. (James 5:14)

We must be careful not to mislead anyone to believe that the oil within itself has any power to heal or cure. But the command to anoint one with oil in the name of Jesus, praying and believing Him to heal or deliver that person was in itself a blessing that promised *transferred power!*

The use of oil was employed, no doubt to remind us that it is not by man's might, nor by his power but by my Spirit (says the Lord) that people are healed. Oil in the scriptures is also representative of the Holy Spirit. Mankind has the awesome and sacred privilege to be a vessel of transferred anointing!

This blessing was passed on to the Church just as it had been given to Israel. The awesome power of a Holy God is transferred when anointing takes place in His name with faith. It is a ministry that applies to any believer who will exercise Holiness, obedience and faith.

There have been times in our services that I have witnessed the choir singing or the band playing under the anointing and the entire congregation is transformed.

People begin to rejoice, weep and even fall out under the anointing as the entire atmosphere is transformed. This is not a time for preaching...but it is a time to move aside and *let the Spirit have His way!*

One truth that I often express when this type of manifestation takes place, the Holy Spirit has not been given to us to entertain the congregation but empower them. Not just to run, shout, speak in tongues or to put on a show in church but he empowers us to engage in His work, to intervene in society as an effective witness with signs and wonders following

The book of Acts records the amazing signs, wonders and miracles that occurred through the empowered disciples. What was the catalyst for such a demonstration of power? They were endued with power from on high,(anointed by the Holy Spirit) to go forth, preach, heal and deliver and the Lord working with them confirming the word with signs following. (Mark 16:20)

We might sum an anointing in these three things:
1. Being recognized and appointed by God
2. A transfer of authority, power and honor from God
3. A specific call and commission from God

After a thorough study of biblical truths and historical evidence on the subject of anointing ;the best working definition I could come up with is : The power of God coming upon an individual or group to perform a task for God's purposes and God's glory.

To publicly anoint one is also a biblical event which represents a literal transfer of power which God uses men to pass on to one another.

The Need for the Anointing

Psalms 2:2
The Kings of the earth set themselves, and the rulers
take counsel together, against the Lord,
and against his anointed...

If you are a believer in Christ, you have some type of calling on your life. You may be an usher, choir member, musician, leader, teacher or pastor in the church but in order to effectively activate and use your gifts you need the anointing.

Often times in ministry you will encounter opposition.

There is a spirit, an unseen power, on earth that is set against the people and the program of God. It was and still is against God's chosen Israel; it was against all of the prophets, Jesus himself, and all of His followers.

This spirit is alive and well but it is a subtle spirit. It's greatest power lies in anonymity, and is launched by offenses, bitterness, envy, strife and ignorance of God's ways and His word.

This explains why Israel is continuously harassed over their sliver of a nation; their divine mandate to maintain God's property for His Son's soon coming Kingdom-the Kingdom of His *Anointed One- is truly a thorn in the side of Satan himself.* The anointing of God is real and has with it the authority of God himself behind it. It also has all hell attempting to discredit it.

The anointing releases God's power in order that God's promises and plans be accomplished. Unfortunately there are some churches that resist demonstrations of the Spirit, however unwittingly, quench the flow of the Spirit. Knowingly or not these churches encourage those who take counsel against the *Lord and his anointed.*

Those of the world do not understand the ways of God. Spiritual moves and outpourings are foolishness in their sight.

But the world's opinion cannot hinder the flow of God within the body of Christ. Only one thing can hinder the flow of the Holy Spirit and that is the church itself. Jesus said of His visit to Nazareth that He did not do mighty works there because of their unbelief. He said to the Pharisees,... "Ye made the commandment of God of non effect by your traditions. I often wonder could this be the reason why there are so many powerless, churches and believers today?

Tradition can be a killer of the flow of the Holy Spirit because man almost always resists altering his religious traditions. This resistance boils down to the question of who is in control?

The Pharisees were overly concerned on one occasion and ask of Jesus "why do thy disciples transgress the tradition of the elders?" (Matt.15:2)

We must understand that every fresh move of God brings a certain transgression of religious tradition. The walls of man-made ritual always crack whenever the wind's of God's Spirit begin to flow.

There is power, joy, energy and anticipation in the manifested anointing of God. Yet, this does not mean every person in that presence will be touched and commissioned. Nor can we predict where He will manifest His presence next. By His sovereign will, God decides when, where and upon whom He will pour out His anointing.

Who Will Receive?

Matt. 5:6
*Blessed are they which do hunger and thirst after
righteousness: for they shall be filled.*

From these words of Jesus we understand that everyone who is hungry for more of God, who will press in to touch God, will be blessed. This being a sovereign move, some of who are not aggressively seeking God's flow will be swept in, but others standing on the outside may be left "on the outside." Many Christians resist moving in the flow of God as they say "I'm not sure this is for me or if God wants me to have something He will give it to me." This is not necessarily true. Energy must be invested and desire exhibited in anything of values. Nothing just happens.

The Scriptures say that all who hunger and thirst will be filled. Some who are not hungry may also be brought into the experience of the fresh anointing, others may not. God is not dictated to by anything other than His own will, and He has only promised to fill those who hunger. He has also instructed us to seek, to ask, and to knock to express our hunger. Those who do so will be filled. Those who don't may or may not. Can you afford to take that chance? Whenever God is pouring out His Spirit, every saint should actively seek an infilling to insure their work in Him will be complete.

The Anointing You Possess

1 Sam. 16:13
Then Samuel took the horn of oil, and anointed him in the midst of his brethren: and Spirit of the Lord came upon David from the day forward.

Many of you are just like David; you posses a powerful anointing yet with no appointing. Don't be discouraged. Remember. It's just a matter of time.

Your anointing is post-dated. I think most of us understand post-dated.

That means you can't cash this until a future date.

Consider David: There he stood in the palace before the King a shepherd boy with a king's anointing; A premature, postdated anointing.

He felt like a fish out of water, completely out of place.

Some of you haven't been able to figure out what's wrong with you. You've been accused of being overzealous, too serious and /or emotional about your calling.

82

But the problem is your anointing is post-dated and you're too anointed to be anonymous.

A kings anointing on a kid— folk think you're putting on. They'll begin to refer to you as the arrogant one but you're not arrogant, just confident.

They say "it doesn't take all that". But consider this. They just don't understand for they are not carrying the weight of a nation's future on their shoulders as you are!

You've got more anointing for what you need right now. God has anointed you for your future not for where you are now but for where you're going. It's postdated anointing.

That's why the devil is trying to take you out now. He knows you're anointed for a greater purpose and it's going to usher you into a greater dimension of your life and open doors for multitudes of others.

You don't understand it yourself. It keeps you happy, shouting, pressing, pushing, praying, hoping, and persevering.

He's anointed you for something that hasn't even happened yet; but *it's just a matter time.*

The Power of the Anointing

Isaiah 10:27
And it shall come to pass in that day, that his burden shall be taken away from off thy shoulder, and his yoke from off thy neck, and the yoke shall be destroyed because of the anointing.

Like Jacob, you may be struggling with who you are. Many today are wrestling with their past. You need to know that there is a place with God of yoke-breaking anointing.

Observe these two scriptures for some timely truths concerning the power of the anointing.

Behold, how good and how pleasant it is for brethren to dwell together in unity!

It is like the precious ointment upon the head, that ran down upon the beard, even Aaron's beard: that went down to the skirts of his garments;

As the dew of Hermon, and as the dew that descended upon the mountains of Zion: for there the LORD commanded the blessing, even life for evermore.(Psalm 133:1-3)

And it shall come to pass in that day, that his burden shall be taken away from off thy shoulder, and his yoke from off thy neck, and the yoke shall be destroyed because of the anointing. (Isaiah 10:27)

We must understand that the anointing flows from the head down. Jesus is the head. Christ meaning= the anointed one. (All anointing flows from Him-downward.)

His set man or woman of the house is second in this order. In order to be recipients of the anointing we must be (aligned or in fellowship) with Him.

Secondly we must be in fellowship (aligned) or see eye to eye with our appointed headship. Please understand the Lord will not circumvent His set headship to give instructions or anoint another before speaking to the appointed and anointed head.

The anointing will be "as the dew of Hermon". The Israelites knew the dew of Mt. Hermon fell heavy in an appointed place. Even in dry weather! Therefore if you are in alignment and submission it is so designed to take authority over your situations "for there the Lord commands the blessing".

According to Isaiah the anointing will lift burdens from you shoulder and take away yokes that have caused you to say and do things and even go places you really didn't desire. The destruction of the yoke is paramount! It isn't enough just to lift it from your neck for if you leave a yoke enabled, it can and will resume it's previous position at any time; But the power of the anointing dismantles everything the enemy had planned for your life.

I am reminded of an incident in the days of the Judges (1 Sam. 5:1-4) when the Philistines stole the ark of the (covenant)God. They brought it from Ebenezer to Ashod and set it up in the house of their god Dagon. (the Philistine fish God)

The presence of God in the ark caused Dagon to fall on his face. The Philistines set him up again and the presence of God caused him to fall a second time. The second fall caused his head and both palms to be cut off upon the threshold.

Everything satan planned to do (his head) and all the things he wanted to do (his hands) has been destroyed by the anointing. He has been cut off and rendered helpless.

Understanding Kingdom Keys

There is something intrinsic about the human psyche that will always have us leaning toward human logic. It sort of leaves us open to the carnal perception of things and if not careful we will find ourselves tossed to and fro by our present circumstances.

This phenomenon is what makes it necessary that we have a true and deep relationship with the Holy Spirit. As we commune with Him we are enabled to tap into a divine perspective that will empower us to operate in Kingdom authority.

It's the power of the anointing that becomes evident in our lives and we no longer fear the gates of hell for when they do rise up against we know they shall not prevail for we have a master key, which is the anointing of the Holy Ghost. This master key prevents us from being locked in or out. We have immediate access.

These are the keys that Jesus promised to Peter. They will and have been a mystery to many but if you are in tune with the Holy Spirit the same mystery becomes an awesome message of prevailing authority to those who understand the code.

Case and point. When Jesus asked the disciples, "Who do men say that I the Son of man am? (Matt. 16:15)Who do you say I am? Only Peter was able to respond with a divine under-standing. "Thou art the Christ, the Son of the Living God." Jesus confirmed that he(Peter) was exposed to an anointing that left the gates of hell powerless against this Divine revelation.

It's when we recognize and confess Jesus as the Christ, He gives us this same master key as was given Peter (the anointing and revelation) to unlock any crisis in our life.)

Please understand the anointing does not prevent the gates of hell from coming against you but it does prevent them from prevailing against you.

May we ever cry out for an infilling of the Holy Spirit that we might be enabled to so commune and fellowship with Him that we walk in and experience a greater anointing.

Discerning the Times and Seasons of life

ECCLESIASTES 3:1-3

The words of the Preacher, the son of David,
king in Jerusalem.
Vanity of vanities, saith the Preacher, vanity of vanities;
all is vanity.
What profit hath a man of all his labour which he taketh
under the sun?

The word Ecclesiastes is Greek for the English word preacher... The Hebrew translation is Goheleth or one who addresses an assembly with philosophical poetry. The author of this sacred writ Solomon or Limuel and is deemed and titled the wisest man who ever lived. Solomon is the son of and successor to King David who also contributes heavily to the book of proverbs.

As you observe the book you will notice that Solomon is airing for the believer his own frustration with life. He starts off in chapter one saying that everything is meaningless. He's come to this level of frustration because he's lived a life that was selfish and sensual. He had everything but lost everything gratifying himself. So in Ecclesiastes Ch.1 he declares to the listener in the Hebrew context of this text; not that life is meaningless but it's like a vapor. For it's here one moment and the next moment everything you worked for, if it was not for the glory of God-will disappear.

He moves forward in Ch.2 to say that even pleasures are meaningless. And wisdom that was not gained from God is vanity; and even a good time is a waste of time if the good time didn't focus on giving God the glory.

But as we observe Ch.3 he begins to submise for us the greatest philosophical question of eternity. What is life? And he tries to deduce for us very carefully and critically what life means and what life represents and he declares unto us 14 issues that we cannot ignore. And from these 14 issues you notice that he does a strange thing. He gives us 7 positives and 7 negatives. Note how they cancel one another out.

In Vs. 2-8 he shares with us 28 things –28 seasons of life that every person will go through and endure 28 issues that everybody from 8-80 will have to experience in their lives.

But note as there are 28 issues we have to deal with in life there are only four seasons. Therefore if we divide the 28 by the 4 and it gives us a quotient of 7.

Seven is the number of totality or completion. So in every full life I'm going to find out that there is a time to live and a time to die—a time to weep and a time to laugh—a time to get and a time to lose- a time to love and a time to hate.

One that doesn't recognize that there is a seasonal mandate for change in life is somebody who subscribes to fatalism. Don't think you're going to laugh all the time or be on top all the time. If so then you don't understand life and you're in for some tremendous disappointments.

Anyone whose ever visited a hospital and went into a critical care unit and saw someone hooked up to a machine and their life being monitored…you see lines going up and lines going down… and a constant beeping sound…but when the lines shifted and flat-lined, or went straight across the screen and the beeping sound turned into one solid continuous sound; that means the patient is dead.

But know that even when God begins to bring you into a shift in life that means a season is about to end and another is about to begin. Each time you experience one of these changes in life God is reminding you that you are still alive but He is in control.

So my beloved there is no reason for you to be depressed over a temporary season of life. You have to remind yourself that this too shall pass!!!

Some body is going through a storm right now but you need to shake yourself and say to yourself when you fell like crying—you feel helpless—hopeless—depressed—in a situation and no way out—you've gotta preach to yourself "baby this too will come to pass". You might need to say to yourself right now—As broke as I am — this too shall pass–lonely as I am—frustrated as I am this too shall pass.

Solomon serves warning to all of us that everything in the spiritual and natural will have to have its course. The brightest day has to relent itself for a cloudy day. The cloudiest day has to move itself for the sun to come back again. When the rain falls nature knows that *it's only a matter of time* before the rainbow shows up. The same rain will be reciprocated into a midst of vapor to form another cloud only to fill and burst to empty itself to the earth again.

Take a note from the wise preacher—it's a trick of the enemy that he plays on the believers to have them think that a season of life is permanent situation. No matter what you're going through it's only a season. Don't get trapped by the instant but tell your-self it's only for a season. This too will pass. Wait a minute and let's thoroughly examine that statement.

It means even if you're on top right now, it's only for a season. If everything is going your way right now it's only for a season. So some of you who become so self righteous and judgmental when the saints begin to shout and praise and call out to God as they go through trials you may look at them and say "all that's unnecessary". That's because you're in a good season now; But just stand still, for what goes up must come down and what goes down will come around...

That's why you ought to make Psalm 34 your theme song—You need to learn to bless the Lord at all times, let His praise continually be in your mouth; especially in the good times for when bad times come you're already warmed up and ready to put the devil under your feet with a Halal (crazy) praise... sometimes you're positioned to offer a praise of total abandonment.

In this proverb of Solomon there are some insightful and philosophical but very critical principles presented for our understanding.

Vs. 1: There's a season for everything and a time for every purpose or matter-under heaven. Now as we matriculate through this life things are going to happen but I truly believe what is going to give the believer the edge is to be able to decipher or discern the difference between a season and a time.

Now a time is a specific hour —where as a season is a general period. The problem with so many believers today is they are constantly prophesying "it's my season"—but nothing ever happens for they are not able to discern a specific time within the season.

So as a bonafied, blood washed, born again believer, I'm not just looking for a season for God to bless me but I have a scriptural right to give God a time.

Psa. 27 says in the *time* of trouble He would hide me—Psa. 47:1 says He's a present help in the *time* of trouble... Psa. 50:15 says call upon me in the *time* of trouble and I will deliver thee. What am I saying—I've got to be bold enough and have faith enough to charge God to be an on time God. "Lord it's 12 noon and by 4pm this eve, I need a breakthrough". But to say Lord I need a blessing in this season could mean I need Him to show up within the next 90 days. But is there anybody reading this book that's desperate enough to say like Smokey Norful in his song? God I need you now... Not another second, not another minute, not another hour of another day.... But Lord I need you now!

If you're someone who is depressed for you feel like you're running late and you needed something to happen for you last month –last year—5-10 years ago and it hasn't happen yet. The problem may be that you didn't give God a deadline. Somebody is tired of waiting, you know your time is running out for you're just that close to give up on church-walking out of your marriage—relationship—your job! But I want to encourage you today to know that your time is not His time—God doesn't operate in kronos—but he operates in cosmos— so even when it looks like you're running late God says *"be still and know I'm God*—it may look like it's late but I'm still running ahead of schedule."

Ask Abraham and Sarah—the 3 Hebrew boys, or Daniel and they'll tell you... He's an on time God.

So he says in Vs.1 there is a time for everything; that's dealing with possession and feeling. But there is a season for every activity and that deals with purpose. Don't miss this... Therefore the gift that you have is given for a season. That's why you can't afford to procrastinate and keep putting things off because you only have a time to do what you've been gifted to do within a season. You could miss your season. That's why some folk who used to be on top aren't there anymore for they outlived their season. They didn't understand that the changing of the guard was taking place. That's why Solomon closes out this book by urging and admonishing us to *Remember thy creator in the days of thy youth*...your season is passing.

Saints you must value the time you have and use it to the max for if you don't use it God will give it to someone else. That's why I don't need anybody to beg me to work in my purpose. When I understand what my purpose is. I just need one half of an excuse to put my purpose into operation. Please don't dare tell me you've been called to preach and not even witnessing to people next door, on your street, job—row. You overlook opportunities to visit hospitals, prisons, missions—and you're only considering a pulpit. Your season is passing you up. As you have opportunity you must walk in your purpose and maximize your moments.

Looking at Vs.2 : He states there is a time to be born and a time to die then he sets up the scenario so that you will understand that you are not invincible, nor eternal—neither are you in control of your time for they've already been set.

Any mother knows that there is a season when you can become pregnant. But there is a time that you must deliver. So you must figure out what season or trimester of the pregnancy you're in. Therefore I can approximate my time of delivery. Can I spiritualize this? Many of you are looking for God to bless you with a harvest and you're not even pregnant yet. But when you're pregnant with purpose and potential you nurture it until it's time to bring it forth. But if you fail to give your baby proper prenatal care—and you have no idea what season of your pregnancy you're in...this could be fatal for you and the gift...the purpose you're carrying.

Seasons of Preparation

Your assignment will require much patience and time for preparation.

The wise King Solomon lets us know that to everything there is a season, and a time to every purpose under the Heaven.

You must also recognize God doesn't call the qualified but He qualifies those whom He calls from eternity.

All the things that you have gone through from childhood to this present time God was training and preparing you. Don't discount your life's journey for it is just as important as your destiny.

Consider some of the other anointed people before you:

Moses was a protégé for 80 years

Joseph spent years in prison before the palace appointment.

David trained many years as child in the sheep fields.

Paul a Pharisee invested years of preparation for his generation.

Even Jesus spent 30 years preparing before launching His ministry.

Various Seasons

<u>Seasons of chastening</u>—"for whom the Lord loveth He chasteneth and scourgeth every son whom He receiveth" Heb. 11: 6

<u>Seasons of isolation</u>—"at my first answer no man stood with me, all man forsook me: I pray God it not be laid to their charge" 2 Tim. 2:12

<u>Seasons of credibility</u>—"endure afflictions, do the work of an evangelist, make full proof of thy ministry" 2 Tim 4:5

<u>Seasons of persecution</u>—"yea, all that will live godly in Christ Jesus shall suffer persecution" 2 Tim. 3:12

<u>Seasons of injustice</u>—"Alexander the coppersmith did me much evil: the Lord reward Him according to His works" 2 Tim. 4:14

<u>Seasons of solitude</u>—"greatly desiring to see thee, being mindful of thy tears, that I may be filled with joy" 2 Tim. 1:4

<u>Seasons of suffering</u>—"if we suffer, we shall also reign with Him: if we deny Him, He shall also deny us" 2 Tim. 2:12

<u>Seasons of warfare</u>—"thou therefore endure hardness as a good soldier of Jesus Christ" 2 Tim. 2:3 "fight the good fight of faith, lay hold on eternal life"…1 Tim. 6:12a

<u>Seasons of disappointment</u>—"for Demas has forsaken me, having loved this present world and is departed…" 2 Tim. 4:10

<u>Seasons of affliction</u>—"but be thou partaker of the afflictions of the gospel according to the power of God" 2 Tim. 1:8
"it is good for me that I have been afflicted; that I might learn thy statutes" Psa. 119:71

As I look back over the years of my life, I can now identify and distinguish the seasons. I understand that each season had it's own purpose. Even though while going through it, I felt totally abandoned by God; but yet I was ignorant of the purpose of the specific season.

Yes. Often times we look at the course of our lives and things seem to be somewhat chaotic. You started out on a straight course but now that same course seems to be completely off course. This is the time when we must really begin to not only trust God from a distance but to earnestly seek him each day. To stay in close fellowship with him that we might know his commands, hear His voice but also become familiar with his ways. Remember our times are in His hands.

The Times and Seasons of Life
Maximize Your moments-Time Is Fleeting

	Individual (Spiritual	Household And Moral	The Church Influence)	God's Kingdom
Seasons and Adventures of life	Preparation: Study Hospitality Business	Production: Babies/ Business Hospitality Elder/Father	Provision: Business Spiritual Father Mentor	Protection: Family Father Hospitality Business
Spiritual Realm Progression of Growth 1Cor.13:11	Child Speaking	Young Man Understanding	Father (Elder) Thinking	Spiritual Father Maturity/ Demonstration
Natural Realm Progression of Growth	Child-Teen Submission Obedience Responsibility Accountability	Parent Responsibility Accountability	Grandparent Posterity Heritage	Great Grandparent Patriarch Matriarch

	Influence (Conscience)	And Impact (Generosity) Economics Education	In each (Truth) Relate truth to Everyday life	Season (Justice) Righteousness Lifestyle
20yearAge 0	20	40	60	80

Segments

(Segments from :"Seasons of Life seminar"
Christian Life Workshop by Greg Harris)

GOING FOR THE ROSES

11 Cor. 12:7
*And lest I should be exalted above measure through
the abundance of the revelations, there was given
to me a thorn in the flesh...*

One spring morning I sat on my front porch enjoying the cool breeze and my favorite cup of coffee; a beautiful multi-colored rose garden caught my eye. It was in full bloom. It seemed to summons me and sure enough I was enticed to pick some fresh roses for a bouquet. As I walked across the front lawn to the rose garden and as I reached into the bush I was interrupted by a sharp sting. It was from a thorn. As I quickly withdrew my hand from the bush and began to nurse my wound I was reminded that thorns are the things we encounter when we reach for the "Roses of Life". Thorns are things that bother us when we strive for the best in our daily activities.

It is the little painful things that we must hurtle and over-come. Just as beautiful as the perfectly sculptured rose may happen to be there is always a thorn present on it's stem, which can injure you. Likewise, as we strive for excellence in life, we are constantly confronted with many petty negative experiences, which prick and injure us in all of our efforts.

Yes. It is the small things that too often trouble us and cause us discomfort.

It is not the boulders that irritate us...it is the small pebbles in our shoes...

It is not the eagles that perturb us...it is the mosquitoes of life...

It is not the clod of dirt we worry about...it is the particle of dust that gets in our eye...

It is not the gigantic, or the colossal, the titanic or the monstrous things that occasionally happen to us. It is the small, insignificant, the minute and the minor things that continue to happen over and over and over again that make up our damaging thorns. In spite of the size of our petty problems, these thorns trouble and irritate us to no end. They are the small irritations, which cause us the most discomfort and the greatest frustrations.

Thorns are individual burdens that cannot be avoided or transferred. After the fall if man the Garden of Eden, thorns became one of the penalties of sin and disobedience. If there had been no sin; there would not be any thorns; but we are all apart of the human condition and must tolerate the frailties and vulnerabilities of life.

Everyone has thorns. No matter how happy people may seem, they still have their thorns. No matter how rich people may be, they still have their thorns. No matter how handsome or attractive, they still have their thorns. No matter how popular, they still have their thorns. Therefore we must always be careful that we don't make other people miserable with our thorn. We don't lead other people to feel sorry for us because of our thorn. Always remember what Jesus said in Luke 16:10, "He that is faithful in that which is least is faithful also in much: and he that is unjust in the least is unjust also in much". Our 'thorn' is given by God; therefore we must bear it with dignity. 2 Corinthians 3: 5 records a declaration of Apostle Paul to the Corinthian church: "Not that we are sufficient of ourselves to think as anything of ourselves; but our sufficiency is of God;" this announcement was to be later tested by a 'thorn' that would constantly trouble him as he preached the gospel.

Apostle Paul, the great preacher of the New Testament, had his 'thorn' in the flesh and he asked God on three occasions to remove it. God's answer, "My grace is sufficient". My strength is to be made manifest not in human strength but in human weakness. Furthermore, Paul began to realize that his 'thorn' was indeed beneficial. It prevented him from being exalted above measure because of his ministerial success. With all the success that he would attain in preaching the gospel, the 'thorn' would serve as a constant reminder that it is God who supplies his power through His sufficient grace.

Thorns may come in many different sizes; but they all have one thing in common. They have sharp points on them that cause pain when in contact with them. God, in his wisdom, has chosen to use thorns simply because thorns:

...can accomplish what nothing else can
...can provide what nothing else can.
...can get one's attention like nothing else can.

God's purpose in thorns is to get our attention, to reach us and teach us

...the sufficiency of God's grace...
...the trustworthiness of God's word...
...and the availability of God's power...

Thorns make us slow down; and think twice before we act, that we go about things in the right way. We need direction in our paths. Thorns will sometimes require us to prayerfully acknowledge the Lord as he directs our paths. Thorns will sometimes make us more compassionate and understanding of the shortcomings of our brothers and sisters. Thorns prevent us from becoming too settled in this world. They make us know that it is better to put our trust in God than 'Put confidence in man'. 'Thorns' may be one of God's ways of reminding us of the curse of sin.... 'Thorns' may be one of God's ways of helping us mature in righteousness and holiness. 'Thorns' may be one of God's ways of getting our full attention, so that he might teach us. 'Thorns' may be one of God's ways of revealing to us just how fragile life is.... 'Thorns' may be one of God's ways of helping us realize that we still need God. Perhaps the greatest lesson of the thorn is patience. Although, there is nothing too hard for

God to do, yet in his wisdom, he may choose not to immediately do things for us. While living in a "hurry up" world, we must cultivate the grace of patience. "In your patience possess ye your souls." (Luke 21:19) We must patiently tolerate the 'Thorns' that God does not remove; relying upon His grace to give you the strength to help you reach for the roses.

Be it an ache or pain in your body that is yet to be healed, a scar from an accident or the healed incision of a past surgery, a physical birth defect, or hindering handicap, a nagging temptation from Satan that you must struggle to overcome, an unfriendly neighbor or the demanding foreman on your job, a family member that has brought disgrace upon your home. Whatever your 'Thorn' may happen to be; just trust God's amazing grace to be sufficient in your conflict. Don't allow the 'Thorns' to stop you from reaching for the "Roses of Life". "Press toward the mark for the prize of the high calling of God in Christ Jesus." (Philippians 3:14) When you get to the point where it seems that you can not go on; and you are troubled on every side, yet not distressed; perplexed, but not in despair; persecuted, but not forsaken; cast down, but not destroyed; (2 Corinthians 4:8-10). Remember, God's grace is sufficient to give you power over your thorns.

The 'Thorns' of life may prick us sorely, but God has the ointment that will heal our injuries. There is a "Balm in Gilead;" and a physician there.' (Jeremiah 8:22) The grace of God will 'bind up your wounds, pouring in oil and wine'.

Healing takes place but remember it's a process which means *it's just a matter of time...*'s (Luke 10:34)

"Let us therefore come boldly unto the throne of grace, that we may obtain mercy, and find grace to help in time of need." (Hebrews 4:16) Wait on God's help; He will give you the grace to go on in spite of the 'Thorns'. Isaiah 40:31 tell us, "But they that wait upon the Lord shall renew their strength; they shall mount up with wings as eagles; they shall run, and not be weary; and they shall walk, and not faint."

Keep on reaching for the roses and let every victory become a testimony of God's sufficiency. In spite of the 'Thorns' keep reaching for the roses.

Some of the greatest gospel songs that have ever been written have been the results of 'Thorns'... some of the greatest testimonies that have ever been told have been as the results of 'Thorns'. Some of the greatest prayers that have ever been prayed, have been the results of 'Thorns'... some of the greatest blessings that have ever been received, have been as the results of 'Thorns'... some of the greatest victories that have ever been won, have been as the results of 'Thorns'... some of the greatest sermons that have ever been preached, have been as the results of 'Thorns' and most of all, some of the greatest saints that have ever lived only became what they were as the results of 'Thorns' in their flesh.

Keep pressing on; God is near to help you. God will take care of you, and God still answers prayers. Keep reaching for the "Roses"... endure the pain and hurt. Your healing is in the plan, you will become successful, and *it's just a matter of time.*

God's Pre-cut Plan - A Pattern

Romans 8:28

This passage assures those of us who love the Lord and know that we have been called according to His purposes that all things are working together for our good.

Yes, the bitter and the sweet; when there's clarity or chaos. Even when it seems like we are the subjects of a mad man who gets pleasure from the erratic display of events in our lives. But with God, this is not the case. There is a reason to the riddle.

I am reminded of the days when my Grandmother Rose used to embroider. I would sit at her feet and look up from the floor and ask what she was doing. She informed me that she was embroidering. I told her it looked like one awful mess from where I was sitting. And from the underside I watched her work within the boundaries of a little round hoop that she held in her hand. I complained again. "It still looks messy to me." She would smile, look down at me and say go outside and play and when I'm finished with it I'll call you and let you see the finished work.

It was confusing because she would use dark threads and then some colored ones, then some bright ones. They looked so jumbled up from my view. A while would pass and then Grandma would call me in to show me her finished work. To my surprise I would see a beautiful multi-colored flower and or a beautiful sunset. I could not believe it because from underneath it looked so messy and unorganized. Grandma would explain. From where you were underneath, it did look so messy and jumbled, but you didn't realize that there was already a pre-drawn plan, a pattern that could only be seen from my side.

Many times through the years I have looked up to God and said, "Father, what are you doing in my life. Things are so mixed up and confusing. My days looks so dark and dreary, please send a little sunshine in my life."

Then God seems to tell me just like Grandma did, "my child, you just go about your business, doing my business, and one day you'll see the finished product, from my side; It will amaze you!"

The Psalmist in Psalm 27: 14 encourages us to wait on the Lord and be of good courage for he shall strengthen your heart.

Knowing God's divine purpose for your life is one of the greatest assets and enablement's to understand and make sense of the perplexities and complications that we encounter.

It's from this premise that Joshua is writing. He's taken a band of men and looked over into the Promised Land.

He's tasted of destiny and has become a partaker of a prophecy that is yet to come to pass. He has caught a glimpse of the promise land.

He's seen it but can't have it, can't live in it, possess it, or move in yet.

Can't unpack yet, but he has to come back across the wall

and go back down to dealing with normal ordinary, stubborn, rebellious, slothful, people.

He's frustrated. Why? He's seen too much!

What he's seen in his spirit just doesn't line up with what he sees in his present life.

He sees greatness but has to live in weakness; he sees destiny but exist in a life of poverty.

Surrounded by people that don't believe; he questions God. "Why did you let me see it and not give it to me?" Can you relate? "Lord you wake me up at 3 AM and showed it to me and then make come back down to live in this mess. Why do I have to wait?"

If you're still reading this book I know that there is unborn greatness in you. I can even feel your frustration if you have to walk with people who do not know neither can comprehend what you've seen. You have to do a job that you've lost passion for. Your passion is in your future but your life is in your present.

You're asking how can I get my passion that has moved ahead of me, to wait on my present, to reach my future? You're wondering doe's anyone else here understand this kind of frustration?

Lord how long will my passion be there and my place be here?

How long Lord must my future be put on hold because of a visionless, faithless people. How long?

But you must practice patience and wait. Remember what happened to Moses?

He tried to accomplish God's means in his flesh and it cost him another 40 years set back. Not by power, nor by might, but by my Spirit says the Lord. Wait, wait I say on the Lord. But you say, "how long?"

Waiting for the Manifestation

Isaiah 40:31
But they that wait upon the Lord shall renew their strength…

Waiting for the vision to materialize can be a trying task in itself. It will painfully frustrate you if you don't learn how to wait patiently for it.

People are fascinated with progress. We like to "make time." We invent ways to "beat the clock." From the electric washing machine to hand held PDA's, something about advancement grips us. Email arrives in mere seconds; laptop computers allow us to work between destinations; microwave meals, delivery services, and drive thru windows provide almost instant gratification. We like to keep moving in life. That's what grips us; the desire to move, to progress. We may see merit in stopping to smell the roses, but we don't like to linger long. But then, life takes us through seasons of pain, doubt, questioning, and suffering, forcing us to wait for resolution.

At times waiting is difficult; a man trying to support a family of five on a disability check, substantially smaller than he is accustomed to, angrily questions, "Where is God? What has he done for me lately?'

His posture; chin set hard, eyes averted, back straight, arms folded tightly across his chest communicates he's in no mood for trite answers. Abruptly he stops talking and drifts inside himself. Softly, eyes averted he says, "If it were not for my kids I would have thrown in the towel a long time ago." He unfolds his arms and drops his head and says to himself "I'm tired of waiting on God."

Most of us can identify with his emotional and spiritual exhaustion at one time or another.

Bills mount, children rebel, friends betray, emotions rage, and hearts ache. Life's relentlessly cold winds appear only to blow on the ground between our two feet. Crises, challenges, and day-to-day demands nibble away at our confidence and peace, leaving us spiritually and emotionally drained.

A popular verse that most of us have memorized tells us that great benefits come with waiting on God.

But they that wait upon the Lord shall renew their strength; they shall mount up with wings as eagles; they shall run, and not be weary; and they shall walk, and not faint. Isaiah 40:31

The Hebrew word for "wait" here means to twist and bind, like a rope. It describes the strength and vigor gained from binding or from stretching. We gain vitality when we twist and bind our lives to the Lord. It's been said that our strength arises when we wrap our web-like strength around the steel strength of Jesus.

Those who wait, exchange their own weaknesses for His strength. God is our strong deliverer. He is the everlasting God. He never sleeps nor grows tired or weary. From Him, strength arises.

Exhausted by fatigue we find our hope in God. His providence, promises, and peace shout out to us through the mounting "white noise" of our circumstances reviving our depleted souls. When we lack both stamina and strength, God liberally grants all we need for the steady progress and spiritual triumph.

Waiting for the Lord means holding on when you feel you can't. It means plugging the holes in your faith as time passes. It means trusting when everything else says it's doomed.

WAIT

Desperately, helplessly, longingly, I cried
Quietly, patiently, loving God replied.
I pled and I wept for a clue to my fate,
And the Master so gently said, "Child, you must wait".
"Wait? You say, wait! My indignant reply
"Lord I need answers, I need to know why!
Is your hand shortened? Or have you not heard?
By faith, I have asked, and am claiming your Word.
My future and all to which I can relate
Hangs in the balance, and You tell me to wait?
I'm needing a yes, a go ahead sign,
Even a "no" to which I can resign.
And Lord, You promised that if I believe
We need but to ask, and we shall receive.
So Lord I've been asking and this is my cry:
I'm weary of asking: I need a reply!

Then quietly, softly, I learned of my fate
As my master replied once again, "You must wait."
So I slumped in my chair, defeated and taut
And grumbled to God, "so I'm waiting...for what?"
He seemed, then to kneel, and his eyes wept with mine,
And he tenderly said, "I could give you a sign.
I could shake the heavens, and darken the sun
I could raise the dead, and cause mountains to run.
All you seek, I could give, and pleased you would be.
You'd have what you wanted, but you wouldn't know Me.

You'd not know the dept of my love for each saint;
You'd not know the power that I give to the faint:
You'd not learn to see through clouds of despair
You'd not learn to trust by just knowing I'm there;
You'd not know the joy of resting in Me
When darkness and silence were all you could see
You'd never experience that fullness of love

As the peace of My Spirit descends like a dove'
You'd know that I give and save for a start,
But you'd not know the depth of the beat of My heart.
The glow of my comfort late into the night,
The faith that I give when you walk without sight,
The depth that's beyond getting just what you asked
Of and infinite God, who makes all things last
You'd never know, should your pain quickly flee,
What it means by "My grace is sufficient for thee."
Yes, your dreams for your loved ones overnight would come true,
But Oh what a Loss, If I lost what's pre-destined in you!
So be silent, My Child, and in time you will see
That the greatest of gifts is to get to know Me.
And though oft' may my answers seem terribly late,
My most precious answer of all is still, "Wait."

                                       Unknown

The Tri-fold Formula for Waiting

God has given us a great vision for the Greater Mount Calvary Church and The Whole Truth Ministries in Manassas and Catharpin, Virginia. He's moved us forward and increased us by leaps and bounds in a very short period of time.

We've witnessed the mighty Hand of God transform a little Church and the side of the road into an international, non-denominational, multicultural, multifaceted, teaching and training institution serving infants to college grad students. To God be the Glory, for we are truly grateful for the Great things He's done. I don't in any way mean to sound like an ingrate; but please allow me to say that according to the Vision there is so much more to accomplish. It is written.

I know God is able! I'm a living witness and a testimony of what God can and will do! But there are times when even I, the visionary, feel so disgusted and frustrated with the present day progression toward the vision. Sometimes I feel like giving up. But it's through the personal and pass experiences, I've found that waiting on the Lord requires more than just being still. There is a three-fold formula that the Body of Christ must become aware of in this season.

If we are to successfully complete our mission, overcome frustration and spiritual burnout we cannot become weary in our well doing. We must learn to run this race with patience. I think this formula will encourage you.

I. Courage

Often times we're burdened with real needs requiring solutions, how can we adhere to the Psalmist's exhortation? "Wait on the Lord: be of good courage, and He shall strengthen thine heart: wait, I say on the Lord."

A person waiting on the Lord needs courage. I recently read a story of a senior couple. While walking a mountain trail to get their much-needed exercise they were attacked by a mountain lion. The lion attacked the husband but his wife found a stick nearby; and with a prayer and total disregard of her own safety with a series of swift beats to the head of the lion she made him loose his grip and drove him off into a cowardly retreat. Now that's courage.

Courage is the mental or moral strength to comfort, persevere, and withstand danger, fear, pain, and adversity. Trying circumstances make our inner constitution feel like shifting sands. Physical, moral, and emotional courage come from within.

Emerson observed that every endeavor requires bravery:

"Whatever the course you decide upon, there is always someone to tell you that you are wrong. There are always difficulties arising that tempt you to believe your critics are right. To map out a course of action and follow it to the end requires some of the same courage a soldier needs to fight for an unseen victory. War has its victories, but it takes brave men and women to win them." Faith and fortitude enables us to maintain the course.

II. Patience

The concept of waiting seems almost alien to most of us in this fast-paced, drive through, twenty minutes or it's free society. If we would be truthful about it, most of us lack the sustaining faith required to wait on the Lord. The demand for instant gratification proves detrimental in four ways:

1. Most impatient people are easily angered. Proverbs 14:29
2. Impatient people are usually ill tempered. Proverbs 15:18
3. The loss of temper signifies inner weakness. Proverbs 16:32
4. The lack of restraint accompanies impatience. Proverbs 16:23

Discontentment usually arises out of impatience Ecclesiastes 7: 8-9

The lofty goals we set for our lives don't materialize as quickly as we anticipated, and seem like they never will. We want to give up. Holding on requires endurance.

II. <u>Diligence</u>

Waiting on the Lord is an active process. Waiting requires action. We must continue our known tasks. Customarily, people are inclined to escape the daily pressures of life, but we should fight against succumbing to that proclivity with everything within us. Day by day, we must continue on. We must revive, nurture, and cultivate our will.

Nothing in the world can take the place of persistence and determination. Talent will not; nothing is more common than the unsuccessful man with talent. Genius will not; unrewarded genius is almost a proverb. Education will not; the world is full of educated derelicts. Persistence and determination alone are omnipotent. The slogan "press on" has solved and always will solve the problem of the human race. — — — Calvin Coolidge

Imagine what would happen in our lives if we gird our natural human frailty with God's unlimited supernatural might. Visualize the power of a church filled with people who posses elevated perspective. Picture what would happen to a country inhabited by people with enduring resilience and faith.

Life's events may slow us down. Our physical and emotional strength may diminish, but out spiritual strength should be on the rise. When difficult circumstances seem to halt our progress we can wrap our web-like strength around the steel strength of Jesus and wait for strength to rise.

Put It in Capable Hands

D ear saints of God. Regardless of how confused or frustrated you may be; or how dim and dreary things may appear; you must always remember the outcome depends on whose hands it's in.

If there is one thing that I have come to understand at this junction of my life and ministry. We must not expect a supernatural outcome from a natural source.

<u>In Marriage</u>: All too often marriages become emotionally bankrupt and come to an abrupt end because marital partners are expecting too much from each other. Both partners are human and prone to make many mistakes (just as one's history and background check would reveal) but nevertheless when led by emotions and supernatural expectations we cast our partners into a superficial (god) role and expect them to work miracles to meet our needs and resolve our problems. This is totally unfair and an insult to God when he has exhorted us to cast our cares upon Him for only He knows how and promises to care for you. (1 Peter 5:7)

This is why a relationship with God is so important before you form a serious relationship with any human and be assured that they too (being equally yoked) are relying upon the same Jehovah Jireah (provider) as you. There are some needs that are designed by God that only through a relationship with Him; a supernatural power can be met.

In Ministry: Praise God for all the gifting and anointing in the Body of Christ.

They are needed and most definitely expected to be used to implement the plan of God in His church. But a pastor or leaders expectation should not be geared toward his staff or servant leaders expecting them to work the supernatural.

In ministry we must be careful not expect the Divine from our leadership! They are not gods. Yes, called and anointed by God but not Divine and should not be cast in such roles of expectation! Neither can they walk on water or be expected to.

Just as Paul spoke to the people at Lystra (Acts 14:15) who contributed Divinity unto he and Barnabas. He took the responsibility to divulge their false expectations when he said "stop it ; don't do these things for we are not gods but we are men of like passions just as you".

Jesus tells us that *with men things are impossible but with God all things are possible*
(Mark 10:27).

Therefore we should not lean to our own understanding but in all our ways acknowledge Him and he will direct our paths. (Prov. 3:5-7)

In Money: We must be careful not to cast false hopes and expectations upon finances. We are required to be good stewards of our money but we must understand and teach this generation these things about finances:

There are some things that money can't buy:
Money can buy me an expensive watch but it can't buy me a cheap second of time.
Money can buy good associates but it can't buy me real friends.
Money can buy me real sex but it can't buy me true love.
Money can buy me a fine house but it can't buy me a loving home.
Money can buy me status but it can't buy me character
Money can buy the greatest accolades but in the end it can't say "well done."

Whose hands are you putting your future and destiny in? Be careful that it is not in humanity!

A basketball in my hands is worth about $19
Put it in Lebron James' hands and it's worth about $100 million
It depends on whose hands it's in.

A baseball bat in my hands is worth about $12
In Derek Geters' hands it's worth $25 million
It depends on whose hands it's in.

A tennis racket in my hands is useless
A tennis racket in Serina, or Venus Williams' hands
Is a Wimbledon championship
It depends on whose hands it's in.

A golf club in my hands is a joke
But a golf club in Tiger Woods hands is 4 master's tournaments
It depends on whose hands it's in.

A rod in my hands might ward of a wild animal
But a rod in Moses' hands will part a red sea
It depends on whose hands it's in.

A sling shot in my hands is just a toy
A slingshot in David's hands is a mighty weapon

Two fish and five loaves in my hands makes a couple of fish sandwiches
Two fish and five loaves in Jesus' hands will feed thousands
It depends on whose hands it's it.

Nails in my hands might produce a birdhouse or a doghouse
Nails in Jesus Christ' hands will produce salvation for the world
It depends on whose hands it's in.

I trust by now you see it depends on whose hands it's in.

So put you concerns, your worries, hopes, dreams, fears, frustrations, and your future, your families, loved ones, your relationships all in God's hands.

For it all depends on whose hands it's in.

Allstate may advertise to be the good hands people...

But God is the Best Hands Person.

UNLOCKING THE DOOR
TO YOUR FUTURE

GEN. 22-28

I f you are a sports fan, particularly football; you will notice that every year within the last two weeks, as we get closer to the super-bowl day, the contest off the field between the opposing teams go to new extremes. Every week we get a new bombardment of reports from the sports world highlighting attacks and slanderous statements from one team against the other. They call it trashing... But as it deals with the projection or prediction of the winner it's always based on something that has happened in the pass of a team or the key player such as Jerome (The Bus) Bettis' fumble at Denver's goaline. The failure of Ben Rothlessburger to scramble or the Seahawks defensive line's ability to hold off a much heavier and tougher offense and shut down Pittsburg's running game... But whoever is to win they will be the new world champion titleholders and ring wearers of super bowl ; Every pro players dream is to win the super bowl and wear a championship ring. If one could team accomplishes this be a star player are a no name player— he has an excellent opportunity to be set for his future. Ring, endorsements, bonus' and many other fringe benefits. So it's not just an ordinary game.... the future is at stake here.

But strangely enough as they are fighting for their future each teams is rated and or predicted to win or loose based on their pass.

My brother and sister's I want to share with you today, whenever you're getting closer to unlocking the door to your future, things from your pass will surface. And the things from your pass are never the things you did well but the things that have a looming dark cloud. Often times you are even named and nick-named by pass incidents.

As we look into Genesis: 25:26 we are introduced to a character by the name of Jacob. Jacob has a shoddy pass even from birth; For when birth was taking place he held on to his twin brother's heel and became know at that moment as a heal grabber — (the supplanter)he wanted to hold on to someone else rather coming out by himself. That begins the dark and dysfunctional relationship between Jacob and his brother Esau. As they develop-mature- and grow into spry young teenagers...we find them again.... and Jacob has tricked Esau out of his birth-right...If it couldn't get any worse than this not only does he take the birth-right but now he steals the final blessing that the father has to give before his death.

Jacob dresses up like his brother Esau and puts goat hairs on his arms and fools his father whose eyesight was failing him and tricks him into giving him the blessing. As the mother looks on she realizes that things are going to get pretty hot and heavy between the brothers...so she admonishes Jacob to run — get out of town.... because if your brother gets his hands on you...when he realizes what you've done to him — he will squeeze the life out of you. So finally now in this parricapy...Jacob after many years as a fugitive, in isolation but he's been married to Leah — and married to Rachel. He's broken off on his own now and started his own business; acquired and accumulated tremendous property, wealth, livestock, houses and land But now when it finally seems like life has started to progress, he finds himself having to face his brother Esau. And I want admonish every reader as you engage this chapter please know and understand...no matter how much you progress, no matter how much success you think you may have accomplished—you have not really accomplished success until you can face and make amends for your pass mistakes.

Key # 1 When you can look head on at the issues that you know that you squandered, that you blew—that you messed up…that's when you know that you're a prime candidate for the next station in life that God is trying to get you to.

But you'll notice something intriguing here as the story develops. You'll notice that Jacob when hearing that Esau has located him and is hastily approaching. Jacob crosses a ford (a river crossing) called Jobbok. My dears you have to understand that we have a serious problem here—because Jabbock is the land of promise; the land that God has promised Abraham but Abraham was never able to see it. So we must understand that immediately as soon as Jacob steps into the region of Jabbock…. (the place of the promise)— —he's just on the edge of it –he's not gone too far…but as soon as he comes into the region of the place of promise is when he's faced with the fight of his life. He sends his family and all his possessions over before him and he was left alone.

An angle stands there to oppose his entrance…Now this passage has been mistakenly termed as an issue between Jacob and Esau, but I big to differ. I truly believe it has nothing to do with Esau. This passage that we're dealing with is a sign to every believer that God had an attitude with Jacob—

Key #2.. When you have wronged your brother—God has an issue with you and you have some God problems. Jesus says if you have ought with your brother I don't even want your offering until you get it right with him.

Well Bishop how do I get it right…. go back to key #1 face up…you blew it…#2. Go to him—(Matt. 18:15 get it right)— settle it between the two of you.

So Jacob thought he could enter into the land of promise without settling pass issues—and yet without a fight.

In essence God is saying to him Jacob, your whole life – you've been a supplanter, a schemer, a trickster and swindler a get over con artist… You can do that with people but when you're ready to possess what I have laid up for you there's no way you'll be able to trick me—you're gonna have to fight for it.

Listen—present-day application: Before we actually move into our promise and posses what God has for us there is a need for a self examination and correction where needed.

I know many believers are still wrestling today and you are truly frustrated...because in every other area of your life you've been able to get over or get by. But when it comes to possessing your dream—the things of God—God will never let you trip up into your promise—but he makes you fight for your promise... And many of you have to be honest—the dream—the vision – the future that God has shown you is causing much frustration because you've never had to fight for anything in your life... you've never done it the hard way you've schemed your way through life —Usually when you needed something you knew who to call, who to trick, who to seduced to get it done...but there's an area of your life God will not allow you to skate through...you've got to deal with it...God says this is one area if you're going to obtain this promise...I'm going to make you fight for it...for he wants you to understand that when you get to the level He's ordained for you –you're be anything but soft.. If you get this promise you'll be so hard from the issues that —you'll have a greater sense of value—and protect what He's put in your hands because you'll then know that it doesn't come easy.

That's why I've got no time for haters and people who are jealous and take my anointing for granted because you have no idea how hard I had to fight.... just to get here. People look at the spoils of war— but don't even pause to consider the casualties and cost of war.

Be careful and refuse to let the spirit of jealousy and envy possess you as you observe others coming into the fullness of their blessing and breakthrough.

Please know if you desire their stuff you will have to have to fight their fight... It's a possibility you may not have the anointing or the Grace for that battle.

Are you sure you want what your neighbor has? If you're not use to fighting for anything you may not understand that you have to fight even harder to keep it.

Even though the promise has been given you it's not easy obtained. You must continue to press toward the mark of the high calling that is on your life. As a believer we must never forget God is on our side but the world is infiltrated with evils that want to block and even stop your progress.

Students, if you are to successfully complete your education it is imperative that you continue pressing your way through college and grad school; getting up in the Morn commuting to and fro, often times working but yet dealing with jealous people and a prejudice boss. In a system that operates by double standards and no one is going to listen even if you can prove your charge... But you still must be steadfast and unmoveable to finish your course.

From a personal standpoint I never knew that you only identify your enemies when you state your mission and purpose. It's then that the true enemy rises up to block your progress. But I also learned in the warfare that there are some battles I don't have to fight. The Bible tells us that when a man's ways please God he will make his enemies at piece with him. So when you encounter turbulence on your Christian journey don't be so quick to expel all of your energy and resources trying to resist but concentrate on pleasing God by staying in His will. He'll fight the battle!

You see Jacob is fighting in the region of his promise but not knowing he's already in it. Some of you are fighting for some stuff that you don't know you already have and the enemy is using your fight as a distraction because he knows as long as he has you engaged you can't realize a sense of destiny.

In other words if you don't know what you want...you'll never know when you get it...if you don't know where you're going you'll never know when you arrive. But when you know that you know...you're already blessed...already have favor. I am a kings kid...my father is rich ...I am healed... Greater is He that's in me—I am more than a conqueror—the victory is mine.

Don't be deceived. What God has for you is for you. It's already shaped up and prepared for you. By all means avoid the propensity to get caught up in complaining, fighting your supervisor, rebelling against spiritual authority. These are tools of the enemy. When you're tempted by these carnal distractions just stop and take time to count the blessings that already surround you. It's already done you must stop and recognize it.

You're already a millionaire—the deposit is just not recorded yet...you're already a graduate you just don't have the degree... Yet...you're already a wife —you just haven't met your husband.... Yet you're already married—you just don't have the ring.... Yet...I'm already a homeowner—I just don't have the address.... Yet...When I'm a person of purpose and destiny— I'm walking around in my anointing and the blessed assurance I've already have it...It's just a matter of time before it manifests.

Jacob enters into the region of Jabbock...and sends away his possessions and sends away his wives... #3. When you enter into your future-and destiny—you must be willing to release what you already have...you must become comfortable with lost. You must learn to sacrifice—that is give up something of value now for something of greater value later. I give it up to prove that the possessions I have –I have them and they don't have me. You see that which you won't give up to God has the propensity to become your God. It's all right to have trinkets, brand name pocket books, designer shoes and clothes but also be ready to depart with them if need be and walk in the confidence that the same God that blessed me with these.... He's able to do exceeding...abundantly...above all that I could ask or think. He has something bigger and better for me!!

#4. Before God brings you completely in to your promise— you've got to learn to reevaluate relationships. Jacob has to send his maid servants away. God wants to deliver you from people and you know that you're delivered when they start leaving you and you don't miss them. (they will leave you)

You're not staying awake all night waiting for somebody to call, to come home, to visit. You must understand that all people are in your life for a season but some just for a season....but the wilderness season of your life is designed for you to walk alone. It's a time that you really learn to lean and trust in the Lord. A time that you validate your testimony that the Lord is your shepherd who will supply all of your needs.

It's in these times also that you have to face the unknown and the unseen. Jacob is alone now...and has to wrestle with a man he can't see.

I can assure you if you haven't there will come a time a situation or place in life where you know you are up against something but you just can't see what you were dealing with... but it's just a matter of time you'll understand it better.

Give God Time to Work

S ometimes those things we desire the most may take longer to achieve. The greater things in life take longer to process and manufacture. For instance, it takes longer to make a Rolls Royce automobile than a Schwinn bicycle even though they are both at the top of the line in their field of transportation. Therefore the greater your dream the longer it takes to achieve.

Many great visions and inventions have been dashed against the rocks of impatience. We must give God time. He specializes in creating and brining things into existence in the right time.

God could have redeemed mankind the very day Adam sinned. But He first gave a Messianic promise in Genesis 3:15 and it began with the words "I will." Therefore if God wills it, whatever He wills, "it" shall be done. It's just a matter of time.

Matthew's gospel (1: 1-17) lets us know that Gods plan entailed establishing a root, which became a people, which became a nation. From Abraham 's generation to the birth of Christ was 42 generations.

The apostle Paul let's us know in Galatians 4:4 that in the "fullness of time" God sent forth His son as the redeemer.

So through it all remember God is working all things to the good for those who love Him and are called according to His purposes. (Rom. 8:28)

Something good is happening that you do not see but wait patiently and joyfully with great expectations.

If you become confused, frustrated, ready to give up, wondering what's going on, why all the turmoil and chaos you're experiencing, don't presume anything, ask God, why?

He definitely has a plan that is yet to be revealed. You must remember that God is a supernatural God and eyes have not seen, ears have not heard, neither has man even thought of the things that God has in store for those who love him. But He reveals them through His Spirit.

Remember the prophet Habakkuk who lived in troubling times? The crumbling society in which he lived roused him to fierce indignation. Perplexed and discouraged by all the corruption that surrounded him he begin to ask God questions like, where is justice? Where is righteousness? Where is the Lord?

Because of his trust in the Lord Habakkuk believed heaven had an answer to his problems. He came to God with his complaint and waited on God for the answer.

When God revealed the big picture to His troubled servant, the prophet was at first shocked, then frightened, and finally bowed the knee in worship. Failing to comprehend God's ways, Habakkuk acknowledged God's wisdom, goodness and power and resolved to trust him no matter what.

Habakkuk (2: 1-2) speaks an encouraging word to us concerning the manifestation of our visions.

The vision is yet for an appointed time, but at the end it shall speak and not lie; though it tarry wait, for it will surely come. It's coming.... it's coming....

Can't you just hear Joshua asking?

How long do I have to wait? I saw the land. We're well able to take it. Why not now... why do I have to wait?

Yes. In all things we have to learn how to wait patiently on the Lord. For God has divinely purposed all things to happen in order and sequence that his purposes are met and His plan is executed according to His divine will.

Even as we observe creation, there was a divine order, a pattern...as Noah built the ark (Gen. 6:13-16) God gave a divine order, a pattern.

As Moses built the tabernacle (Exo. 25: 9-22) God gave a divine order, a pattern.

As David returned the ark of God to Jerusalem the city of David (2 Sam. 6) there was a divine order, a pattern.

Even as Solomon the son of David built the temple (1King: 6) there was a divine order; a pattern. God is a God of order, sequence and timing.

Identifying and Removing Delays

The scripture let's us know that God is not a man that He should lie, nor the son of man that He should repent, if He said it shall He not do it? If He spoke it shall He not bring it to pass? (Num. 23:19)

Many are saying yes, I believe all of that and I also know that the promises of God are yea and amen in him ...but.

How long must I wait before I see my prayers answered, my vision come to fruition? That type of response could be revealing a spirit of anxiousness.

Joshua and Caleb had to wait...40years. But they did posses the land. It was just a matter of time.

I'd like to encourage you by these words of truth "every delay is not a denial."

I think the prayer of serenity is appropriate for these times.

Let's pray it together now –
Lord grant me the serenity to accept the things I cannot change,
The courage to change the things I can, and the wisdom to know the difference...Amen.

We must take the responsibility of identifying and removing the delaying factors of our own destiny.

Offenses:

Then said he unto the disciples, It is impossible but that offences will come: but woe unto him, through whom they come! Luke 17:1
    Jesus teaches his disciples that it is impossible to live in this world without being offended. Then why should we act as if some strange thing happened to us?
    The question the believer should ask him or herself is how will I respond to the offense; not if, but when it comes?
    A wrong response can delay your breakthrough to destiny.

In John Bevere's book *"The Bait of Satan"* he identifies to the Body of Christ this most subtle and entrapping device of satan called offense.
    Quote: "Anyone who has trapped animals knows a trap needs one of two things to be successful. It must be hidden, in the hope that the prey will stumble upon it, and it must be baited to lure the animal into the trap's deadly jaws.
    Likewise satan the enemy of our souls, incorporates both of these strategies as he lays out his most deadly and deceptive traps. They are both hidden and baited.
    Satan along with his cohorts is not blatant as many believe. He is subtle and delights in deception. He is shrewd in his operations, cunning and crafty. (His power is in anonymity)
    Don't forget he also disguises himself as an angel of light. If we are not trained by the Word of God to rightly divide between good and evil, we won't recognize his traps for what they are.
    One of his most deceptive and insidious kinds of bait is something every Christian has and will encounter...OFFENSE. Actually offense itself is not deadly- if it stays in the trap. But if we pick it up and consume it and feed on it in our hearts, then we have become offended. Offended people produce much fruit...such as hurt, anger, outrage, jealousy, resentment, strife, bitterness, hatred and envy. Other consequences of picking up an offense are insults, attacks, wounding, division, separation, broken relationships, betrayal, and backsliding."

Often those who are trapped in this device do not even realize they are trapped. They are oblivious to their condition because they are focused on the wrong that was done to them. They are in denial. The most effective way for the enemy to blind us is to cause us to focus on ourselves.

The first law of discipleship that Jesus gives His perspective followers is self denial. (Luke 9:23)

Unforgiveness:

Matthew 11: 24 Therefore I say unto you, What things soever ye desire, when ye pray, believe that ye receive them, and ye shall have them.
25. And when ye stand praying, forgive, if ye have ought against any: that your Father also which is in heaven may forgive you your trespasses.
26. But if ye do not forgive, neither will your Father which is in heaven forgive your trespasses.

If you don't give it —then you don't qualify to receive it.

We live in a culture where we don't always mean what we say. But I am a true believer of Christ. Which means I believe He said what He meant, and meant what He said without any exceptions. We must take His word seriously. He walks at a level of truth and integrity that transcends our culture or society.

Therefore if he says: "if we do not forgive one another, neither will our Father in heaven forgive us our trespasses." We must take Him for his Word. He meant it!

Too many Christians want God to forgive them for their trespasses but they have failed to forgive those who have offended them. Not understanding that the way we forgive, release and restore another person is the way we will be forgiven, released and restored and ultimately launched into our personal destiny.

And forgive us our debts, as we forgive our debtors.
Matt. 6:12

Bitterness

Let all bitterness, and wrath, and anger, and clamour, and evil speaking, be put away from you, with all malice:
And be ye kind one to another, tenderhearted, forgiving one another, even as God for Christ's sake hath forgiven you.
Eph. 4: 31-32

If we hold on to offenses and allow unforgiveness to dwell in our spirits we then set our hearts up to become calloused and overtaken by bitterness. Bitterness then turns to hate and hate begins to turn on the he holder and activates a self destruction component.

Bitterness always results in self-inflicted wounds.

I am reminded of Joseph who had many opportunities to be bitter because of the wrongs he suffered. Gen. 40: 4-15

His brothers sold him into slavery, Potiphar's wife lied and entrapped him,

Pharaoh's cupbearer lied to and forgot him and left him imprisoned two years after he interpreted the cupbearer's dream.

It is very clear that a series of serious misdeeds was done to Joseph. He obviously did not see a prison or any detour for that matter in his dreams. Yet God was totally in control as long as Joseph did not get in the way by becoming bitter.

Joseph's future stayed intact because he did not allow bitterness to encage him. The only thing that would have confined him would be to entertain bitterness.

Joseph was greatly used by God in the midst of all these discouraging circumstances. He displayed Godly and mature behavior. His response to his conditions and circumstances later proved to be beneficial in elevating him to a position only second in the kingdom.

Please remember if you are harboring bitterness for any reason Rid yourself of it by confessing to God and forgiving your offender. Get over your hurts. Hurt people only hurt other people...but ultimately hurt themselves and their God given purpose. Bitterness is a destiny killer. It thwarts the plan of God for your life.

Forgive and release; you then will be forgiven and released to move into your future.

He the Son sets free is free indeed!

Pride

The sin of pride is the sin of sins. It was this sin, we're told, which transformed Lucifer, an anointed cherub of God, the very "seal of perfection, full of wisdom and perfect in beauty," into Satan, the devil, the father of lies, the one for whom Hell itself was created. We're warned to guard our hearts against pride lest we too "fall into the same condemnation as the devil."

It was the sin of pride which first led Eve to eat of the forbidden fruit. In Genesis we read, "Then the serpent said to the woman, 'You will not surely die. For God knows that in the day you eat of it your eyes will be opened, and you will be like God, knowing good and evil.' So when the woman saw that the tree was good for food, that it was pleasant to the eyes, and a tree desirable to make one wise, she took of its fruit and ate. She also gave to her husband with her, and he ate."And who do you think was that serpent of old who first introduced Eve to this sin of pride? It was none other than the devil himself, eager to share his condemnation with others.

St. Augustine of Hippo (354-430 A.D.) wrote, "Pride is the commencement of all sin' because it was this which overthrew the devil, from whom arose the origin of sin; and afterwards, when his malice and envy pursued man, who was yet standing in his uprightness, it subverted him in the same way in which he himself fell. For the serpent, in fact, only sought for the door of pride whereby to enter when he said, 'Ye shall be as gods.'"

Sin Of Pride - Preoccupation With Self

The sin of pride is a preoccupation with self. It is thus very fitting that the middle letter in the word is "i." Pride is all about "me, myself, and I." So even as the word "pride" is centered upon an "i," the sin itself is also centered upon "I."

We read of Lucifer's fall, *"How you are fallen from heaven, O Lucifer, son of the morning! How you are cut down to the ground, you who weakened the nations!*

For you have said in your heart: 'I will ascend into heaven, I will exalt my throne above the stars of God; I will also sit on the mount of the congregation on the farthest sides of the north; I will ascend above the heights of the clouds, I will be like the Most High.' Yet you shall be brought down to Sheol, to the lowest depths of the Pit." (Isa. 14:12-15)

Satan's enmity against God began with "I". And so it is with us. If you are preoccupied with yourself, you are suffering from the sin of pride.

One way to determine whether or not you are preoccupied with yourself is to evaluate your motives. Take the pursuit knowledge for example. If you study hard because that's what the Lord wants you to do and you're being obedient to Him, that's good. That's obedience to God. Or if you study hard because you want to become a teacher so that you can edify others and help them to grow, that's good too. That's love for others. But if you study hard solely to amass knowledge for yourself, just so you can say that you know more than everyone else, that's bad! Your focus is upon yourself and your own glory. That's preoccupation with self. That's pride. And if this is the case for you, not only are you already suffering from pride, you're setting yourself up to be totally consumed by it! The Apostle Paul wasn't joking when he said, "Knowledge puffs up, but love edifies." And anyone who is ever been there will tell you, knowledge for the wrong reasons (i.e. personal glory) *will* lead to a proud heart and enmity against God.

Sin Of Pride - An Attitude

The sin of pride is rightfully distinguished as the foremost among the seven "deadly sins," each of the seven equally as deadly (Proverbs 6:16-19), but none quite as notorious as this "sin of the devil."

It is most beneficial for the servant of God to look at this sin of sins: how it manifests itself in our thoughts and lives, what are its effects and how we are to fight against it taking hold in our hearts.

We must observe how this sin in Biblical history took it's awful toll on those that committed the sin of pride and how they're portrayed in the Bible. It's important to observe how pride manifested itself in their lives and form these observations seek some divine strategies and make some practical changes in our behavior that we may overcome it's silent and subtle attack and infect our own hearts and minds. Finally, we each must commit to combating the sin of pride with the practical application of the word and humility.

Humble yourselves in the sight of the Lord, and he shall lift you up. James 4:10

Likewise, ye younger, submit yourselves unto the elder. Yea, all of you be subject one to another, and be clothed with humility: for God resisteth the proud, and giveth grace to the humble.

Humble yourselves therefore under the mighty hand of God, that he may exalt you in due time: 1 Peter 5: 5-6

Some hurts, habits, and hang ups have been with us for some time and aren't easily overcome overnight. It is a process. But we must make the choice to forgive now and continue to seek God for divine guidance in removing them and the patience to wait for Him to remove those hindrances that are designed only for divine intervention and removal.

Jesus admonishes His disciples one occasion to let the wheat grow up with the tare and when harvest time comes He would assign reapers to do the separating.

As we look at the historical record and the biblical account of the Exodus we can identify two reasons they had to wait as long as they did.

<u>First</u>— all of the negative voices around them were perpetuating the situation by saying what couldn't be done. Unfortunately they had to wait until every voice of doubt to die or be removed.

Therefore every anointed believer who is desiring to see the promises of God fulfilled in their lives will have to become comfortable with death and efficient in eulogies and be prepared to conduct one over every voice of doubt and fear that's been holding you back from the promises of God...

Yes. You must commit that bad company and relationship to the ground... Ashes to ashes – dust to dust. There are those who are actually speaking death over your vision when they speak negative and faithless words. How can two walk together except they agree? (Amos 3:3)

The Company You Keep

Y ou must learn to wisely choose your company and not let it chose you. It's been said that is better to be alone, than to be in the wrong company. You can determine your destiny by evaluating your close friends.

If you run with wolves, you will learn to howl and devour.

But if you associate with eagles, you will learn sour to great heights.

Each day that God blesses you with life you ought to look to heaven, thank Him and then make your way to a mirror and affirm yourself by saying "I believe I can fly-for I believe in me."

Yes, you must believe in yourself. The Bible says as a man thinketh in his heart so is he Proverbs 23:7; and he shall have whatsoever he sayeth. Mark 11:23.

But remember a mirror only reflects a man's face, but what he is really like is shown by the kind of friends he chooses. The simple fact of life is that you become like those with whom you closely associate…for the good and the bad.

An important attribute of successful people is their impatience with negative thinking, speaking and acting people.

Some people are called to do the good and others to do the great. So as you begin to do great and mighty exploits some of your associates will surely change.

Some of them will not, others don't want to and others cannot attain the heights that you are called to.

Many will want you to remain on the same level with them and instead of climb they will want you to crawl.

It is better to be alone than in the wrong company. Tell me who your best friends are and I will tell you who you are. If you run with wolves, you will learn to howl. But if you associate yourself with eagles, you will learn to soar to great heights.

The less you associate with some people, the more your life will improve. Any time you tolerate mediocrity in others, it increases your mediocrity. An important attribute in successful people is their impatience with negative thinking and negative acting people. As you grow in the Lord, your associates will change.

Your true friends will stretch your vision, while your true enemies will choke your dream. Those that don't increase you will eventually decrease you.

Consider this:

Never receive counsel from unproductive people.

Never discuss your problems with someone incapable of contributing to the solution, because those who never succeed themselves are always first to tell you how. Not everyone has a right to speak into your life. You are certain to get the worst of the bargain when you exchange ideas with the wrong person.

Don't follow anyone who's not going anywhere. With some people you spend an evening: with others you invest a lifetime.

Be careful where you stop to inquire for directions along the road of life.

Wise is the person who fortifies his life with the right relationships.

The second reason their time was extended in the desert is they wouldn't let Moses die.

Moses must die for he represents the former order. What Moses did was good for then but it won't work now.

Idols had to come down, sacred cows had to be killed, images and groves had to be torn down.

God knew that this was so important to their effective transition to their place of promise that upon the death of Moses He personally funeralized and buried him and never divulged to this day the whereabouts of his grave to the people of Israel.

It would have been a great distraction and a hindrance to the people's transition.

This represents old allegiances to people, places and things that God Himself has removed, forsaken and or disapproved of.

The Joshua generation brought in with it new paradigms for ministry.

Until you divorce from unprofitable old allegiances and sacred cows and dedicate yourself to hearing a fresh word and receiving a vision from God, or faithfully supporting the vision of your man or woman of God, you too may be hindered and put in a holding pattern of repetitious failures and unfulfilled dreams.

It's difficult to do 21st century ministry with horse and buggy methods.

I am reminded of a story told in the gospel of Mark Chapter 1.

A man sick of the palsy has need of healing; four of his concerned friends put forth a combined effort to get him to Jesus for they heard he was in the town of Capernaum preaching and healing again. Together they got the sick man to the house where Jesus was located but because of the enormous crowd they could not get him in the presence of Jesus.

They begin to think and came up with an out of the box, unconventional way of accomplishing their mission. They made their way to the roof and uncovered it and made a new entrance and lowered their friend into the presence of Jesus. It worked! Not only did the man receive his healing but Jesus acknowledged the efforts of the team and pronounced that by their faith their friend was healed.

Now this was not only an act of faith by the four men but it must be noted as an effective way of ministry through introducing a new and bold paradigm.

Churches, pastors and parishioners alike must understand that as our mission remains the same, the motive remains the same, the message remains the same, but often the method must change to be effective in ministry.

Doing a self critique

You must do a self-critique and ask yourself the following questions and answer them honestly.

1. Do I have a sense of personal destiny?

Dr. Miles Monroe in his book *in the pursuit of purpose* ... says, "The greatest tragedy in life is not death but life without a reason. It is a dangerous thing to be alive and not know why you were given life. One of the most frustrating experiences is to have time and not know why."

What is my purpose and what am I doing about it?

2. Am I willing to suffer loss to achieve my goals?

If you are to graduate from the pediatrics of Christianity to the level of true championship you must suffer loss of some things.

Be it reputation, friends, invitations, family heritage, customs, and most of all your sense of self-righteousness.

And like the apostle Paul count it all but dung for the excellence of the knowledge of Jesus Christ. Be willing to forget those things behind you. Not from a case of divine amnesia but purposely and intentionally putting some things out of mind for they will only distract you, slow you down, and hinder your race.

3. Am I truly dedicated to moving forward?

In order to progress you can't vacillate back and forth. Quit one day and go back the next. You must be steadfast, unmovable and committed to moving forward. Forward from grace to grace, faith to faith, challenge to challenge, level to level.

Don't practice double-mindedness. James says in 1:6. He that wavers is like a wave of the sea, tossed and driven by the wind. A double minded man (doubter) is unstable in all of his ways. Let him not expect to receive anything from the Lord.

Paul said I must press toward the mark of the high calling of God, which is in Christ Jesus. Let us be mature that consider these things. If not, God will reveal it.

The Promise of God's Presence

Matthew 28: 20
... "low I am with you always, even unto the end of the age..."

R emembering God is never present in a former visitation. Jesus said." As you go, I'll be with you always. Even unto the end of the age."

Don't be deceived by trying to duplicate and imitate what God did in another dispensation, another ministry, and another person's life. He is with "you" now! In this time, this dispensation supplying his grace and power to enable you to be successful.

Did not the Lord speak through the prophet saying?

"In the last days I will pour out of my spirit upon all flesh: and your sons and your daughters shall prophesy, and your young men shall see visions and your old men shall dream dreams.
And on my servants and on my handmaidens I will pour out my Spirit and they shall prophesy." (Joel 2:28-30)

Did not the Lord speak through the prophet Isaiah and say?

"Behold, I will do a new thing, now it shall spring forth; shall you not know it?" I will even make a way in the wilderness and rivers in the desert." (Isa. 43:19)
He will make a way out of no way.
Not by power nor by might but by my Spirit saith the Lord of host.
Zach. 4:6

Remain Committed

Am I truly committed and accountable to validated leadership?

You must understand that what you make happen for others God will make happen for you. Whatsoever a man soweth...that shall he also reap.(6:7)

Don't let the enemy beguile you. You must stay under a covering and remain connected to a higher order. Each act of obedience shortens the distance to any miracle you are pursuing. Each act of disobedience delays your time of arrival at destiny.

How can I be assured that I am committed?

There are many ways to detect an individual's commitment level but I think Jesus gave us the better one when he said you shall know a tree by the fruit it bears.

Become a fruit inspector and inspect for the following fruit in your own life.

One must truly understand the true meaning of a commitment:

A deliberate and calculated choice to steadfastly set your course, with an unwavering obligation, to go above and beyond your original expectation to accomplish a predetermined objective.

Why is it so in the "BC" stage of our loves we understood commitment? But now that we are save, we either have a case of selective amnesia or during the transfer some files were lost. Christians can be the most uncommitted people.

Look at the Muslims, the Jehovah Witness. The Seventh Day Adventist, the Catholics, they hold fast to their commitments regardless of who disagrees or is offended by it.

It's a bad commentary for the body of Christ that we become known as always late, half-hearted, ashamed, frivolous, lethargic, sometime and casually committed!

One who is truly committed must have observed and/or thoroughly processed through the following steps:

Process of Commitment

1. Conviction (by Holy Spirit)

And when he is come, he will reprove the world of sin, and of righteousness, and of judgment: **John 16:8**

2. Confession (Unto salvation)

For with the heart man believeth unto righteousness; and with the mouth confession is made unto salvation.   **Romans 10:10**

3. Conversion (A renewing of the mind)

And be not conformed to this world: but be ye transformed by the renewing of your mind, that ye may prove what is that good, and acceptable, and perfect, will of God.   **Romans 12:2**

4. Compliance (Submission)

Submit yourselves to every ordinance of man for the Lord's sake: whether it be to the king, as supreme;

Or unto governors, as unto them that are sent by him for the punishment of evildoers, and for the praise of them that do well. *1 Peter 2:13-14*

Types of Commitment

There are also five (5) types of commitment:

1. Casual- The type of commitment that is made without much forethought
2. Cohersed- The type that is made under pressure
3. Cunning—that which has a hidden agenda
4. Comradery—I will, if you will type
5. Calculated- The commitment one must make as it pertains to vision

The first four are definitely the ones that will produce negative results; but the fifth one, the calculated commitment is the one where I purposely, intentionally, sit down with my spouse, family, employer and any significant other in my life and explain to them the seriousness of my conviction, my confession, my conversion and most definitely my compliance to the order of God.

Secondly I must consider, plan, and count what it is going to cost me to carry out this new assignment for my life. What is it going to cost me to maintain my loyalty, trust and integrity as it pertains to this endeavor I'm about to enter into?

As a serious believer on a divine mission it is most important for you to establish the cost because commitment itself goes through five (5) stages.

The first being the *Defining Moment:*
This moment is defined when I carefully choose to consider my course of action challenging the outcome.

My defining moment: In 1984 the company I worked for begin to lay off it's employees and finally it reaches me and I was without a job; but soon thereafter the company consolidated or merged with another conglomerate and I was offered the opportunity to transfer to Northern VA. I could have stayed in North Carolina and made a comfortable living but when I was offered the opportunity it was as if I heard a clarion call from God. Get out of this place! Go..take the offer. I couldn't explain it but I truly felt as if God Himself was propelling me into my destiny; Even though the place was totally unknown and foreign to me (as in Abrams case) I was being challenged to temporarily leave my family, home, and my comfort zone. I was toiling with the decision for two weeks when a peaceful spirit came over me and I heard a still small voice saying "everything will be alright my Son."

Twenty five years later now, when I'm discouraged and want to give up or throw in the towel (oh yes, we have those moments as well) but it's that defining moment which sustains and encourages me and it reminds me that the purpose for which I originally came here is a Divine one. It's amazing for after being here six months I received and accepted my call to preach. After evangelizing, five years later I was called into the pastorate.

This path now led me to the: *Decision Moment*:

This was yet another challenge but a decision had to be made. You see I had house notes, car notes, two kids in college and a church that paid me $75 per week. Yes you read it right, $75 per week to start, so you can imagine I had an unhappy wife and discombobulated household. But after much mental anguish, for this didn't make common sense, following was the emotional trauma, for no one including myself could explain how we were going to survive. But, I heard from God again and felt that familiar unction and against all odds, human reasoning and understanding I resigned from my secular job of 15 years to become a full time pastor without full time benefits! But God had a plan. Did I see it? No.

But in less than two years our ministry expanded so quickly we were bursting at the seams. At that time we were receiving an average of over 100 members a year but in a facility that would only accommodate at the max 120 people.

This left us in desperate need of more space...another building, a larger facility we didn't have the funds for either.. What did we do?

Explored our options; we petitioned the county for permits to set up trailers for classrooms and extra space. We were denied. Secondly we ask our neighbors to sell us property for expansion purposes, again we were denied.

What do you do when you don't know what to do? You've tried everything and you've run out of options. We fasted and prayed.

Once again, after fasting and praying for a solution I heard from heaven...the Spirit spoke to me and said "you have problem..but a good one. But it's not your problem... cast your cares upon Him, depend on God and

as for you...write the vision and you continue to speak the vision."

My response was OK Lord. The vision that you have given me is of a larger building with classrooms and spacious seating and a center for our children.

I began to boldly speak it and include it in my sermons.

Little did I know God had already prepared a place for us and placed someone in the congregation whose heart was in tune with the vision and already had the heart for what God desired to do.

This gentleman was a private business owner and entrepreneur, a visionary who I could deeply relate to. The Lord increased his business and caused it to prosper so that he was able to donate all of the funds to purchase another site.

After putting together a transition plan which was implemented very smoothly and timely. Then we established a pre-school and academy, an infant center, with before and after care. We were able to purchase six new vans for transportation, installed an industrial kitchen which enabled us to offer hot meals on daily basis.

Later the ministry took another leap of faith an established a Bible college and an international ministry to Jamaica, WI which we presently serve and support six churches.

All of this happened within two years of my *Decision Moment* to trust God and launch out into the deep.

Yes by trusting God and following this monumental move in my life I became a Founder and Principal then a Founder and CEO, of the Whole Truth Ministries then selected to become a Bishop in the Ecclesia Ministries, International of Chapel Oaks Maryland. No brag, but all I'm saying is that God is able to do exceeding, abundantly, above all you ask or even think…(Eph. 3:20)

All that I wanted to do was to be a good provider, father and husband for my wife and family; but God had an even greater vision for my life.

After being here at GMCCC I have been offered other opportunities to pastor larger churches, to Bishop larger districts or Dioceses but those things were offered to me by great men who I truly respected; but I never heard or felt a Divine call conviction or unction from the Holy Spirit (which I know so well in my present experience) to accept any of these invitations.

Therefore I have kept my course and if I never do anything else, or go anywhere else, one thing I do know is that God set me here and gave me a vision for this people and it's my desire to be faithful over my charge.

Many ask today, "how did you get here"? My answer; I trusted God and the unction of the Holy Spirit. In twenty five years I haven't looked back or suffered

lack; for where God gives a vision he will also give provision.

Distasteful moments: These are the moments when the very people you've been sent to help turn on you. (as Moses experienced) Many get up and leave you because they can't handle the truth that you preach and teach. Neither do they see the necessity to repent from traditional, historical and even ungodly lifestyles and submit to the paradigm, lifestyle and ministry of our Christ. You see often times we are sent to teach people who don't already have a grasp on or thorough understanding of the word.

It was only then that I discovered that many believers and folk who are truly committed to the cause and love the Lord and

His church but they don't understand divine order, protocol, spiritual authority, purpose or vision. These things had to be taught.

People began to rebel and have their own home bible studies. Boycott you on Sundays or get up and walk at when you get up to preach.

I'm speaking of leaders and the people who said they would always be with you but now they are deserting you. These are not only distasteful moments but they are totally disloyal moments.

But I had the promise of God, "I'll be with you". I'm a bonafied witness that if you have a few faithful members and faith in the promise and power of God; that's enough to implement the vision that God gives.

In times like these we must always remember that personal stewardship over our own lives is very important. The enemy will attack; but when the enemy attacks it's never about you but it's about the vision and the move of God.

Yes, He was doing an awesome thing, a new thing. So the enemy retaliates by trying to use the same devices he attempted to use against Nehemiah in days of old to stop the work.
1) Discouragement
2) Dismay
3) Disillusion
4) Defamation
All to try and stop the move of God; But God said "Upon this rock I will build my Church and the very gates of hell will not prevail against it." (Matt.16:18)

As faithful workers in the Kingdom we must be determined and our reply must be that of Nehemiah "I am doing a great work, so that I cannot come down: why should the work cease, whilst I leave it, and come down to you?" (Neh.6:3)

So during these distasteful moments I also discovered that this was my test. Often God will test His servants to know if they can really be trusted and tried.

For the vision is His vision but whatever I do in this time is a direct reflection on Him. So in these moments I begin to understand the importance of trust.

What is this trust? Godly trust… It is willingness, an ability and a resolve to always resist the devil, restrain your flesh and make a righteous choice on a consistent basis. That's why *our journey is just as important as the destiny*. Through our experiences God wants to so temper us that regardless of the pressures, temptation or trials of the distasteful moments we experience His servant will resist the devil, restrain his flesh and make a righteous choice.

The Dying Moment: This is the moment when the tactics of the wicked lose their impact over you. To successfully reach your destiny in God and remain faithful in His service you must die to negative attitudes that will cause you to do several things.

1. To be judgmental of your leaderships decisions. You must refrain from judging the decisions of leaders God has put in your life to lead you.
2. Die to the attitude that causes you to be negative about personality differences and emulate others. Never compare yourself with your leader. Why? Because the scripture teaches that the teacher is always greater than the student.
3. You must die to the attitude of repulsive responses concerning issues that you do not have the authority to even speak about.
4. You must die to the attitude that will cause you to give in to the temptation of personal agendas. Stay with the vision of the house.
5. You must die to the attitude that causes you to have the need of acceptance from people more than the obedience to leadership.
6. Die to the attitude of being dishonest and having unethical practices.

Finally the: *Dynamic Moment*

This moment presents the reality of God's promised benefits of righteousness. They become real to you. Your personal vision becomes a reality.

But we must understand that nothing just happens. We just don't stumble into these dynamic moments. The dynamic moment is the time when you begin to reap what you have sown. The scripture lets us know emphatically that what one has sown, that shall he also reap..(Gal. 6:7) If God has assigned you to a ministry he has placed you there to help the senior pastor or the visionary of that house bring his/her vision to fruition. It is imperative that you find your place of service, exercise your gifts and do so by displaying two very important components that are necessary for success.

Loyalty and Trust:

Loyalty is a necessary component for those who are called to assist others in the implementation of a vision. Habakkuk 2 refers to those who assist as those who read it and run with it.

Now this loyalty must be exhibited and practiced faithfully in 3 vital areas.

1. There must be a certain loyalty one must have to the order of God
2. There must be loyalty placed in the vision that God gives
3. There must be loyalty placed in the visionary-the person to whom God gives the vision to.
4. Now when given an assignment to assist a person who has vision you must understand that you have been entrusted with something of great value and great importance. So we must take a look at vision from God's perspective. How God see's vision. Then we can understand more so the components of loyalty and trust.

   One of the problems in the body of Christ there is not enough loyalty and trust among believers and for the lack of these components we aren't able to do the greater works and mighty exploits that the word of God says we are to do. (Dan. 11:32)

   Churches and Ministries that move forward in Kingdom building understand and are blessed with staff and members of integrity, loyalty and trust.

Loyalty Defined:

A faithfulness displayed in my conduct, conversation and contribution that remains steadfast and unmovable in the face of pressure and any temptation to renounce, to desert, or to betray a person or cause.

Please understand, loyalty is not allegiance. They are not the same. Let me explain. Allegiance unlike loyalty, under pressure will re-align itself to another or a cause for the benefit of itself.

Therefore loyalty is only allegiance until it has been tested, tried, and proven steadfast under pressure.

Loyalty is yet allegiance until it faces some temptation. A temptation to betray, desert, or to renounce and bears up successfully then it can be declared loyalty. Until then it's just allegiance which will align itself to another for the sake of itself.

I can recall taking an oath upon my induction into the U.S. Army. Raising the right hand and affirming to defend this county against all enemies foreign or domestic. (Little do we know we do the same when we take communion and recite our responsive covenant).

Now there are some enemies to vision, foreign and domestic. There are some outside and others inside the house of God. But the in house ones can be labeled as disloyal.

True allegiance is loyalty that not only says but demonstrates it's willingness to die for what it believes in. To give up my natural life before I even entertain deserting, renouncing, or betraying a purpose or a cause.

As we observe Joshua 1:15-18 we are introduced to these components that are lacking and must be restored to the Body of Christ.

15 Until the LORD have given your brethren rest, as he hath given you, and they also have possessed the land which the LORD your God giveth them: then ye shall return unto the land of your possession, and enjoy it, which Moses the LORD'S servant gave you on this side Jordan toward the sunrising.

16 And they answered Joshua, saying, All that thou commandest us we will do, and whithersoever thou sendest us, we will go.

17 According as we hearkened unto Moses in all things, so will we hearken unto thee: only the LORD thy God be with thee, as he was with Moses.

18 Whosoever he be that doth rebel against thy commandment, and will not hearken unto thy words in all that thou commandest him, he shall be put to death: only be strong and of a good courage.

So we must believe in the principles of God and what he's doing in our generation; so much even if it took giving up our natural lives we would.

But we also understand as believers that whatever we give up for the Kingdom will be restored and multiplied back to us. (Mark 10:29-30)

There are two major enemies that will assault and attack you because of your loyalty and commitment to vision or a visionary.

1. Persecution..a malicious intent to drive you away, to scale back your dream, to give up your righteous pursuit. To injure you somehow. That's persecution's aim..to cause you to betray trust and loyalty.
2. Fleshly Desires: Many people give in, give up and throw away their loyalty because of fleshly desires. Throughout the Bible many who were on the path of Grace, Favor and Success by following another...gave it all up and gave in to betrayal of a person or a cause that God wanted to do in the earth through an individual and loss all inheritance because of disloyalty.
3. A disloyal person, an unfaithful person is like a Benedict Arnold in the Body of Christ. A traitor!
4. But a loyal and faithful person is an asset and a commodity in the body of Christ.

Everyone will testify of his own goodness saying "I'm faithful and I'm loyal" but a true follower, faithful and loyal has to be declared so by others. (Prov. 20:6) You can bestow loyalty and faithfulness upon yourself. It has to be declared by someone else.

If I want to know if I can trust you I don't ask you but those around you, those who have dealt with you on various levels. Personal references, track records, and project reviews must be considered.

A steward must be found faithful...a steward is one worthy of trust. (1 Cor. 4:2)
Faithfulness Detected:
A faithfulness that is displayed over three areas.
1) Conduct:

You can't live a compromised lifestyle and be an asset to the vision, or the visionary. You must also be careful not to even be involved in ministry that has not been properly ordained; something that the pastor or leader has spoken against or does not give his blessing and you support it because a friend, kin, or you sense an opportunity for yourself.

This is not loyal. We must be careful to check our company(and it's influence) as well as our conduct.
1 Thess. 5:
21. Prove all things; hold fast that which is good.
22. Abstain from all appearance of evil.
23. And the very God of peace sanctify you wholly; and I pray God your whole spirit and soul and body be preserved blameless unto the coming of our Lord Jesus Christ.

1 Cor. 5:9-11

9. I wrote unto you in an epistle not to company with fornicators:
10. Yet not altogether with the fornicators of this world, or with the covetous, or extortioners, or with idolaters; for then must ye needs go out of the world.

11. But now I have written unto you not to keep company, if any man that is called a brother be a fornicator, or covetous, or an idolater, or a railer, or a drunkard, or an extortioner; with such an one no not to eat.

2 Cor. 6:14-18
14. Be ye not unequally yoked together with unbelievers: for what fellowship hath righteousness with unrighteousness? and what communion hath light with darkness?
15. And what concord hath Christ with Belial? or what part hath he that believeth with an infidel?
16. And what agreement hath the temple of God with idols? for ye are the temple of the living God; as God hath said, I will dwell in them, and walk in them; and I will be their God, and they shall be my people.
17. Wherefore come out from among them, and be ye separate, saith the Lord, and touch not the unclean thing; and I will receive you,
18. And will be a Father unto you, and ye shall be my sons and daughters, saith the Lord Almighty.

2) Conversation:
Luke 6:45
A good man out of the good treasure of his heart bringeth forth that which is good; and an evil man out of the evil treasure of his heart bringeth forth that which is evil: for of the abundance of the heart his mouth speaketh.

The first thing to detect when a person is becomes shaky and disloyal is their conversation. Listen to a person and you can tell where they are, where they've been and where they're going; By his/her conversation. Out of the abundance of the heart the mouth speaketh.

There is an inseparable connection between your heart and your mouth. Many times folk will say what they think you want to hear for they consciously processing everything they say. But when under pressure they are not giving it any real conscience thought and whatever is in the heart proceeds from their mouth. Quickly you will hear "I didn't mean that" but they just really revealed what was in their heart. The tongue discloses the contents of the heart. You can cross circuit the system for so long but under pressure or the choking

Moment comes, whatever is in the heart will come from the mouth.

So we as keepers of the flame, protectors of the vision, guardians of the trust must be careful of what comes from the mouth and be sure we are not negatively talking about or against the order of God.

3). <u>Contribution:</u>
Matt. 6:19-21
19. Lay not up for yourselves treasures upon earth, where moth and rust doth corrupt, and where thieves break through and steal:
20. But lay up for yourselves treasures in heaven, where neither moth nor rust doth corrupt, and where thieves do not break through nor steal:
21. For where your treasure is, there will your heart be also.

Immediately when one hears contribution he begins to think finances. Yes it does include finances but it's not only about your treasure but also includes your time and talent.

If you really believe in something you give to the cause.

The scripture is very clear that where a man's treasure is... there is his heart also; which includes your time, treasure and talent.

I submit unto you that your attendance in what goes on in the body of Christ where you have been assigned is also a issue of loyalty. Just my presence speaks; faithful attendance means I'm truly with this. Getting involved to share my gifts or talent is a part of being a steward; using my God given talent, my uniqueness, my specialty. We all have one or more. We were created with purpose and purpose activated is when I began to exist for a benefit outside of myself.

When I begin to contribute through giving my tithes and offering, using my gifts and talents then I truly become fulfilled. We all have something to give, all of us.

Many believers give up on themselves because of their present conditions never considering their potential or possibilities. Saints you must stand regardless of your circumstances. God is good and he never gives up on us. You may not be living out your created purpose at this time but just remember you're clay in the potter's hands and He's still molding you into a vessel that's fit for use in the Kingdom.

Being confident of this very thing..that he that began a good work in you will perform it until the day of Jesus Christ. (Phil. 1:6)

After proving yourself faithful and loyal and making a contribution to the vision of your house please know that there is destiny set before you for your life and remember it is hidden in another man's vision. It's Just A Matter of Time before it is revealed.

By following the vision of my pastor I found my own purpose. It wasn't my purpose to go get a church or organize one. But my purpose was to find a man that could help me with my call but at the same time I was introduced to his vision which I sought to be an intricate part of by helping and serving to help him with his vision.

I discovered as God sees fit to promote you to something else he'll speak to the set man of the house and or He will speak it through you as you demonstrate loyalty and commitment to the vision and visionary by your conversation, conduct and contribution.

But until then refrain from having a personal agenda. Remain there, and faithfully give your support and loyalty to the order of God, vision of God and man/woman of God.

Remember: For promotion cometh neither from the east, nor from the west, nor from the south.
But God is the judge: he putteth down one, and setteth up another.
(Psalm 75:6-7)

Develop the Mentality Of A Finisher

As I began close this book I was reminded and truly moved by the Spirit to the spirit to include this final thought and admonition.

Finish your course! Whatever you have been tasked to do you must be steadfast, unmoveable and bring it to completion. To do so you must develop the mentality of a finisher.

King Solomon say *"I returned, and saw under the sun, that the race is not to the swift, nor the battle to the strong, neither yet bread to the wise, nor yet riches to men of understanding, nor yet favour to men of skill; but time and chance happeneth to them all."* Ecc. 9:11

When you have been chosen for a task you must realize that it is your time and chance; not depending on swiftness, strength, bread or riches, favor or skill.

But consider God calling you to the forefront for such a time as this. Look unto Jesus who is the author and finisher of our faith and He will provide what is needed to insure success. But we must have a made up mind to complete the journey.

Finish your assignment. During my years of education I experienced many able, intelligent and wise students who failed to graduate because they fail to complete a simple paper or for some unknown reason they just dropped out.

There is an attitude that presently exist in the Body of Christ that needs to be corrected. There is a character flaw that needs to be addressed and corrected immediately...We must stop quitting and quit stopping regardless of the circumstances.. We must become serious about our assignments and finish our course.

I've observed elders, pastors, ministers, deacons and other officers and members who were publicly ordained and covenanted to hold true until the end but all too soon these covenants came to an early resignation. They quit because of rough or difficult circumstances-unfriendly fire or a hostile environment.

The Apostle Paul charges Timothy his son in the faith to "endure hardships as a good soldier of Jesus Christ....Wherein I suffer trouble, as an evildoer, even unto bonds; but the word of God is not bound. Therefore endure all things for the elect's sakes that they may also obtain salvation which is in Christ Jesus with eternal Glory."   (2 Tim. 2:3-10)

Saints we must endure hardships.

Don't get upset when you are rebuked or corrected and change churches when things don't go your way, (it's really not about you anyway) but submit to authority, humble yourself and change your mind. Endure hardships!

You must understand that correction is not rejection but an act of love intended to prepare you for projection...into your future and destiny! Wait for your change to come.

God knows when you're ready and through His Divine unction you will be called, then sent or set into higher ministry by your spiritual authority. Don't go out there on your own. It is totally out of the will of God. You need a covering, a connection you need a Father.

Paul exhorts the believers in Galatians 6: 9 *And let us not be weary in well doing: for in due season we shall reap, if we faint not.*

Now he's not talking about being overcome with exhaustion to the point where you can't go on. But he is talking about being overcome with frustration to the point you choose not to go on. Don't throw in the towel. When you quit you don't abort your salvation but you do lose some of your inheritance. You will be rewarded for your good works! (*For the Son of man shall come in the glory of his Father with his angels; and then he shall reward every man according to his works.*Matt.16:27)

Satan is not omniscient neither does he know the mind of God, nor does he have the mind of Christ; but I do believe with all sincerity that every now and then God allows him to stand on the threshold of our destiny and peep over into our promise land and see what God has prepared for those who love Him...those who are the called according to His purposes.

Yes, satan know it's yours....laid up just for you if you continue to be faithful and the only way to keep you from receiving your reward is to cause you to faint....fall by the way side... quit...give up...throw in the towel.

Just as Jesus told Peter, "Simon, Simon, Satan has desired you that he may sift you as wheat.(Luke 22) But I prayed for you that your faith fail not."

My dear reader. Whatever you do...don't quit. It's too soon to quit! You may be going through some tough times now but remember Paul's exhortation :

For I reckon that the sufferings of this present time are not worthy to be compared with the glory which shall be revealed in us.   *Romans 8:18*

It would behoove each of us to look back and examine our lives. If you see a trail of unfinished projects, un-kept promises, broken covenants. It could be that our destiny is being withheld because we have yet learned to be faithful and to finish our course.

It's late, but not too late to correct this character flaw. Let's develop the mentality of a finisher.

Conduct A Spiritual Audit

1. Your conduct————Godly character, integrity; Is it approved by the word of God?
2. Your conversation—The fruit of your lips. Is it contrary to the word of God?
3. Your contribution—time- talent—treasures—does it measure up to Gods command?

If you answered no to any of these questions your disobedience in any of these areas could be causing the delay in your breakthrough to the wonderful promises of God.

You and only you have the power to change the course of your life. Yes. You can turn it around right now, today by making a decision to repent and change your behavior..

Ask God to forgive you of your disobedience or rebellion. Humbly accept God's forgiveness.

Commit to doing His will today. He is faithful and just to forgive and cleanse you from all unrighteousness. He will receive and restore you into His good graces. 1 John 1:19. His mercy endureth to all generations.

Be encouraged my beloved brothers and sisters. God is doing a new thing, He is pouring out His Spirit in these last days to accomplish His divine will in the earth realm by ushering in His eternal Kingdom. You are a prime candidate to be used mightily of the Lord.

And as you delight yourself in Him and give your time and attention to

do His will, I am a living testimony He will give you the desires of your heart.

It's Just A Matter of Time

Remove the U From Failure

To start "failing forward," you need to look at failure differently.

Do you think of yourself as a failure? Maybe not in every area of life, but in at least one important one? Well, you're not alone. Many people think that having failed makes them a failure. Too many people...

Seeing yourself as a failure is a negative thinking pattern. It doesn't make you feel any better, and even more important, it doesn't help you do any better in the future. To start "failing forward," you need to look at failure differently.

Pick any area where you've repeatedly failed and do the following:

Examine your expectations for that area. Write them down. Are they realistic? Do you expect to do everything perfectly? Do you expect to succeed on the first try? How many mistakes should you expect to make before you succeed? You'll probably need to adjust your expectations to allow many more mistakes or failures before success.

Find new ways to do your work. Brainstorm at least twenty new approaches to your job or task. Now, I should point out that people who fear failure have a hard time brainstorming because they don't want to list a "wrong" idea. Be flexible and list even the most outrageous approaches. Then be even more flexible and try at least half of the ideas on your list.

Focus on your strengths. In areas where you've frequently failed, ask yourself, "What did I do right?" It's normal to focus on what you did wrong in the situation, but everyone has some strengths. Rather than focusing on patching up your weaknesses, determine to use your best skills and personal strengths to maximize your efforts.

Vow to bounce back. No matter how many times you fall down, pick yourself up and keep going. This sounds too simplistic, but it's really essential. Until you commit to keep going, you will always entertain the option of quitting after a failure.

Don't wait until you feel positive to move forward. Instead, act your way into feeling good. And stop defining yourself as a failure. That kind of negative thinking will always block you from failing forward.

John Maxwell

Thoughts and Sayings on Time

Time is a sort of river of passing events, and strong is its current; no sooner is a thing brought to sight than it is swept by and another takes its place, and this too will be swept away. - Marcus Aurelius

Nothing valuable can be lost by taking time. - Abraham Lincoln

Waste of time is the most extravagant of all expense. - Theophrastus

Those who make the worst use of their time are the first to complain of its brevity.

Nobody sees a flower, really - it is so small - we haven't time, and to see takes time, like to have a friend takes time. - Georgia O'Keefe

Don't use time or words carelessly. Neither can be retrieved.

History repeats itself, which is good because most people don't pay attention the first time anyway.

Time is like a river - it flows by and doesn't return. - Chinese Proverb

Time flies...and eternity waits. - Polish Proverb
Time is nothing but erosion on a man's soul. - Dave F.

One thing you can learn by watching the clock: It passes the time by keeping its hands busy.

The secret lies in how we handle today, not yesterday or tomorrow. Today...that special block of time holding the key that locks out yesterday's nightmares and unlocks tomorrow's dreams.

There is more time than life. - Mexican Proverb

Time is nothing more or less than the opportunity to expand and enrich one's soul by doing the same for others. - Ruthi Crockett

Unlike other resources, time cannot be bought or sold, borrowed or stolen, stocked up or saved, manufactured, reproduced, or modified. All we can do is make use of it. And whether we use it or not, it nevertheless slips away.

Time will pass, will you?

The bad news is time flies. The good news is you're the pilot. - Michael Altshuler

Time is infinitely more precious than money, and there is nothing common between them. You can't accumulate time; you cannot borrow time; you can never tell how much time you have left in the Bank of Life. Time is life... - Israel Davidson

Procrastination is the thief of time.

Lost time never returns. - Czech Proverb

An inch of gold cannot buy an inch of time. - American Proverb

Right now a moment of time is passing by...We must become that moment. - Paul Cezanne

People who make the worst use of time may be the same ones who complain that there is never enough time.

Time and tide wait for no man. - American Proverb

Time is the greatest gift of all.

Time is the coin of your life. It is the only coin you have, and only you can determine how it will be spent. Be careful lest you let other people spend it for you. - Carl Sandburg

An airport is where you go to waste time waiting that you're going to save flying.

Half our life is spent trying to find something to do with the time we have rushed through life trying to save.

Lost time is never found again. - Thelonious Monk

Time is a created thing. To say, 'I don't have time' is like saying 'I don't want to...' - Lao Tzu

Until you value yourself, you won't value your time. Until you value your time, you will not do anything with it. - M. Scott Peck

They say that time always changes things, but you actually have to change them yourself. - Andy Warhol

Don't ever think you 'don't have time.' After all, there are 525,600 minutes in a year.

When the most important times are occurring, we don't even recognize them or notice. We are just busy living our lives. Only looking back do we know what was a great moment in our lives.

We need time to dream, time to remember, and time to reach the infinite. Time to be.

Love and time, those are the only two things in all the world and all of life, that cannot be bought, but only spent.

What may be done at any time will be done at no time. - Scottish Proverb

Time is a great legalizer, even in the field of morals. - H. L. Mencken

Time is an invisible web on which everything may be embroidered. - Joaquim Maria Machado de Assis

The time for extracting a lesson from history is ever at hand for those who are wise. - Demosthenes

Most time is wasted, not in hours, but in minutes. A bucket with a small hole in the bottom gets just as empty as a bucket that is deliberately kicked over.

If you want to make good use of your time, you've got to know what's most important and then give it all you've got.....Lee Iacocca

For man also knoweth not his time: as the fishes that are taken in an evil net, and as the birds that are caught in the snare; so are the sons of men snared in an evil time, when it falleth suddenly upon them. King Solomon

Decision page

Are you sure of your salvation?

God's remedy: The cross

God's love bridges the gap of separation between God and you. When Jesus Christ died on the cross and rose from the grave, he paid the penalty for your sins. "He personally carried the load of our sins in his own body when died on the cross". 1 Peter 2:24

<u>Assurance of salvation</u>
Admit your spiritual need. I am a sinner.
Repent and be willing to turn from your sins.
Believe that Jesus died for you on the cross
Receive, by faith—ask Jesus Christ into your heart and life.

<u>Sinners prayer</u>

Dear Lord Jesus, I know that I am a sinner and need your forgiveness. I believe that you died for my sins and rose to assure my salvation. I want to turn from my sins.
I now by faith invite you to come into my heart and life.
I confess. I am saved. I am now a child of God.
Thank-you Lord...Amen

Now that you 're saved

Read and study God's word
Pray everyday
Stand for Jesus Christ and make your life count. Don't be ashamed. Tell others about your decision.

Identify with a bible believing, teaching church for worship, instruction, fellowship and service.

Begin to commit His word to your heart

For God so loved the world, that He gave His only begotten Son, that whosoever believeth in Him should not perish, but have everlasting life.
John 3:16

Ministry helps

If you are interested in receiving CD's or DVD's of any of the following messages please fell free to contact our audio ministry at the address below, telephone us or contact us on the web address.

Bishop Smith would also be delighted to minister at your Church or Ministry affair.

Contact our office at the number below.

The Whole Truth Ministries, Inc.
9514 Westmoreland Avenue
Manassas, VA 20110
Ofc. 703-368-9865— Admin: -703-368-5941 Fax—703-330-2161
Website: www.thewholetruthministries.com or Church web at
www.gmccc.org

Are You Willing to Fight Like men
What Must I Do to Be Saved
Dynamic Christian Living
Living a Successful Single Life
How to Find a Mate
Marriage and Family Life
God's Will for My Life
What to do When Stuck in a Rut
Women on a Mission
The Necessity of a Vision
Making My Vision a Reality

The Theology of Somehow
When the Brook Dries Up
The Catastrophe of Unfulfilled Prophecy
Whom Shall I send—Who Will Go for Us
In Pursuit of Purpose
Discerning the Seasons of Life
Identifying my spiritual gifts
Loosing the bonds of the past
Delivered but not divorced
Don't get trapped by the instant
A level Christianity
The Power of Influence
Leaders Step Up
The Champ in Your Child
The Day Jesus Shouted
The Left Generation
Jesus Will Make You Clean
After You've Been Cleansed
Don't Be Left Hanging
When God Won't Move the Problem
What's That in Your Hand?
When Deliverance Takes Place
The Cost of Discipleship
Unlocking the Door to Your Future
The Trial of Your Faith
Walking By Faith
Your Victory Is In Your Walk
In Need of a Breakthrough
Fasting For Breakthrough
Going To Another Level
Who Is This Baby
The Opinon That Really Matters
This May Be My Last Chance

CPSIA information can be obtained at www.ICGtesting.com
Printed in the USA
BVOW030953070312

284561BV00002B/1/P

9 781602 665828